Learning Grunt

Monitor and automate complex JavaScript tasks
and processes by obtaining a practical understanding
of Grunt

Douglas Reynolds

BIRMINGHAM - MUMBAI

Learning Grunt

First published: March 2016

Production reference: 1210316

Published by Packt Publishing Ltd.
Livery Place
35 Livery Street
Birmingham B3 2PB, UK.

ISBN 978-1-78588-880-9

www.packtpub.com

Credits

Author
Douglas Reynolds

Reviewer
Justin McCandless

Commissioning Editor
Amarabha Banerjee

Acquisition Editor
Sonali Vernekar

Content Development Editor
Riddhi Tuljapurkar

Technical Editor
Danish Shaikh

Copy Editor
Tasneem Fatehi

Project Coordinator
Sanchita Mandal

Proofreader
Safis Editing

Indexer
Mariammal Chettiyar

Graphics
Disha Haria

Production Coordinator
Nilesh Mohite

Cover Work
Nilesh Mohite

About the Author

Douglas Reynolds is a web application developer. He holds a degree in software engineering and has worked with web technologies for over 15 years. Douglas currently works for *Herff Jones* as a Senior Web Applications Developer as a member of a highly skilled and dedicated team of professionals. Douglas writes and lectures on web technologies, teaches at Illinois State University in the Department of Technology, and writes on topics of technology for *Packt Publishing*. Douglas and his wife of over 20 years, along with their son and two dogs, live in Bloomington, Illinois. He loves his family and friends and enjoys spending time outdoors in nature, riding his Harley, and continually developing his relationship with God.

Acknowledgement

Thank you, Lord, for the blessings in my life and providing me with what I need. I would like to thank Packt Publishing for giving me this incredible opportunity to write my first complete book. Having a published work has been a goal that I have thought about for many years. Special thank you to Sonali, who approached me with this idea and helped me take my first steps to begin writing and sharing information to help others learn. I have worked with a group of amazing people that have provided support and guidance to me on this project. I would especially like to thank Riddhi and Usha for their valuable cooperation and support. Justin's attention to detail and brilliant ideas helped me to refine the content into what I truly believe will provide a valuable resource to learning Grunt as well as a reference to return to again and again. Additionally, my most heartfelt thanks go to my beloved family, my wife Patricia, my son Zachary, and our dogs Penny and Juno (they spent countless hours accompanying me at my desk).

Once you make a decision, the Universe conspires to make it happen

–Ralph Waldo Emerson

About the Reviewer

Justin McCandless is a software engineer and a build-process nerd originally from Las Vegas. He has studied electrical engineering at the University of Michigan before spending several years working abroad in Latin America and China. He now resides in San Francisco and works as a full-time engineer at *Teespring*. He enjoys contributing to the programming community through the open source platform, technical writing, and mentorship.

www.PacktPub.com

eBooks, discount offers, and more

Did you know that Packt offers eBook versions of every book published, with PDF and ePub files available? You can upgrade to the eBook version at `www.PacktPub.com` and as a print book customer, you are entitled to a discount on the eBook copy. Get in touch with us at `customercare@packtpub.com` for more details.

At `www.PacktPub.com`, you can also read a collection of free technical articles, sign up for a range of free newsletters and receive exclusive discounts and offers on Packt books and eBooks.

`https://www2.packtpub.com/books/subscription/packtlib`

Do you need instant solutions to your IT questions? PacktLib is Packt's online digital book library. Here, you can search, access, and read Packt's entire library of books.

Why subscribe?

- Fully searchable across every book published by Packt
- Copy and paste, print, and bookmark content
- On demand and accessible via a web browser

Table of Contents

Preface

The essence of workflow automation is an exemplification of at least two of the three great virtues of a programmer.

> *There are three great virtues of a programmer: laziness, impatience, and hubris.*

> *—LarryWall, Programming Perl (1st edition), Oreilly And Associates.*

Larry Wall went on to explain that laziness is the quality that makes you go to great effort to reduce overall energy expenditure. Grunt provides task automation to relieve the developer of the mundane, repetitive processes that occur during software development. Expending effort up front with Grunt will pay dividends in reduction of energy expenditure in the development lifecycle. Impatience, Larry Wall said, makes you write programs that don't just react to your needs but actually anticipate them. Grunt automation can react to your needs by responding to events, such as file changing. With the right combination of tasks and configurations, Grunt automation can even seem as if it is anticipating your next step. *Learning Grunt* aims to provide you with a ramp from getting up and running to developing your own Grunt plugin. If you are at all lazy and impatient, in the context of a virtuous programmer, then *Learning Grunt* has been written just for you.

What this book covers

Chapter 1, Grunt Dependencies, will let us know that Grunt is a Javascript task runner, the purpose of which purpose is task automation. Before we can get started with Grunt, we need to make sure we understand and implement Grunt's prerequisites.

Chapter 2, Foundation for Creating an App using Angular.JS, will create a sample application to use throughout this book with the Angular-Seed scaffold.

Chapter 3, *All about Grunt Plugins*, introduces a sampling of common Grunt plugins, overview of their purposes, brief examples of implementation, and additional references and information.

Chapter 4, *Configuration of Grunt Tasks*, As we became familiar with installation and configuration of Grunt tasks. Focus is placed on two main files in a Grunt project; package.json and Gruntfile.js.

Chapter 5, *Task Setup in the sample_project Application*, defines the sample_project automated build process, introduces user stories, and then covers Gruntfile.js configuration from top to bottom.

Chapter 6, *Building the Sample Project*, will explain the process of loading tasks. We check functionality to ensure we get the expected results, and create custom and default tasks in order to automate the build process.

Chapter 7, *Advanced Grunt Concept*, will help you create your own custom task. Learn how to use the Grunt plugin tool and then write a custom Javascript plugin to Gzip files into a deployment directory.

What you need for this book

Any modern Windows, Linux, or Macintosh computer, a text editor, command-line or terminal interface, and an Internet connection will meet the requirements of this book. Node.js is very lightweight and requires a minimal amount of RAM. The sample project will require approximately 500 MB of storage, although 1 GB of storage is recommended.

Who this book is for

If you are a JavaScript developer and want to learn project monitoring and automation using Grunt, then this book is for you. Basic knowledge of Node.js and Angular.js is assumed. However, no previous experience using Grunt.js is required.

Conventions

In this book, you will find a number of text styles that distinguish between different kinds of information. Here are some examples of these styles and an explanation of their meaning.

Code words in text, database table names, folder names, filenames, file extensions, pathnames, dummy URLs, user input, and Twitter handles are shown as follows: We can include other contexts through the use of the `include` directive.

A block of code is set as follows:

```
[default]
exten => s,1,Dial(Zap/1|30)
exten => s,2,Voicemail(u100)
exten => s,102,Voicemail(b100)
exten => i,1,Voicemail(s0)
```

When we wish to draw your attention to a particular part of a code block, the relevant lines or items are set in bold:

```
[default]
exten => s,1,Dial(Zap/1|30)
exten => s,2,Voicemail(u100)
exten => s,102,Voicemail(b100)
exten => i,1,Voicemail(s0)
```

Any command-line input or output is written as follows:

```
# cp /usr/src/asterisk-addons/configs/cdr_mysql.conf.sample
    /etc/asterisk/cdr_mysql.conf
```

New terms and **important words** are shown in bold. Words that you see on the screen, for example, in menus or dialog boxes, appear in the text like this: "Clicking the **Next** button moves you to the next screen."

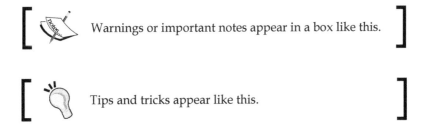

Warnings or important notes appear in a box like this.

Tips and tricks appear like this.

Reader feedback

Feedback from our readers is always welcome. Let us know what you think about this book—what you liked or disliked. Reader feedback is important for us as it helps us develop titles that you will really get the most out of.

To send us general feedback, simply e-mail feedback@packtpub.com, and mention the book's title in the subject of your message.

If there is a topic that you have expertise in and you are interested in either writing or contributing to a book, see our author guide at www.packtpub.com/authors.

Customer support

Now that you are the proud owner of a Packt book, we have a number of things to help you to get the most from your purchase.

Downloading the example code

You can download the example code files for this book from your account at `http://www.packtpub.com`. If you purchased this book elsewhere, you can visit `http://www.packtpub.com/support` and register to have the files e-mailed directly to you.

You can download the code files by following these steps:

1. Log in or register to our website using your e-mail address and password.
2. Hover the mouse pointer on the **SUPPORT** tab at the top.
3. Click on **Code Downloads & Errata**.
4. Enter the name of the book in the **Search** box.
5. Select the book for which you're looking to download the code files.
6. Choose from the drop-down menu where you purchased this book from.
7. Click on **Code Download**.

Once the file is downloaded, please make sure that you unzip or extract the folder using the latest version of:

- WinRAR / 7-Zip for Windows
- Zipeg / iZip / UnRarX for Mac
- 7-Zip / PeaZip for Linux

Errata

Although we have taken every care to ensure the accuracy of our content, mistakes do happen. If you find a mistake in one of our books—maybe a mistake in the text or the code—we would be grateful if you could report this to us. By doing so, you can save other readers from frustration and help us improve subsequent versions of this book. If you find any errata, please report them by visiting http://www.packtpub.com/submit-errata, selecting your book, clicking on the **Errata Submission Form** link, and entering the details of your errata. Once your errata are verified, your submission will be accepted and the errata will be uploaded to our website or added to any list of existing errata under the Errata section of that title.

To view the previously submitted errata, go to https://www.packtpub.com/books/content/support and enter the name of the book in the search field. The required information will appear under the **Errata** section.

Piracy

Piracy of copyrighted material on the Internet is an ongoing problem across all media. At Packt, we take the protection of our copyright and licenses very seriously. If you come across any illegal copies of our works in any form on the Internet, please provide us with the location address or website name immediately so that we can pursue a remedy.

Please contact us at copyright@packtpub.com with a link to the suspected pirated material.

We appreciate your help in protecting our authors and our ability to bring you valuable content.

Questions

If you have a problem with any aspect of this book, you can contact us at questions@packtpub.com, and we will do our best to address the problem.

1
Grunt Dependencies

Grunt is a JavaScript task runner. As its name alludes, this tool performs the grunt work of completing development tasks, which might include linting JavaScript, running tests, generating minified JavaScript and CSS, moving files and directories, creating archives, and the list goes on and on. In fact, the purpose of Grunt is task automation, which means running one or more tasks with the least amount of user interaction needed in order to complete the work. Almost any task can be automated with Grunt and many plugins (tasks) already exist that can be installed and used in your project. It is possible to write and publish your own plugins to meet the need of tasks for which a plugin does not already exist. You can also modify existing plugins to meet project-specific requirements. The Grunt community is very large and there is a great deal of documentation and resources available as a result. With a minimum amount of research effort, information on specific Grunt topics can be found in a wide range of places. This book, for one, will provide information on the installation and setup of Grunt, installation and configuration of tasks found in the **Node Package Manager** (**NPM**) registry, creation of custom tasks, Grunt API documentation, and much more. Some main benefits of using the Grunt task runner are that Grunt task automation improves productivity by handling repetitive tasks with efficiency, reduces errors using automated processes, and lessens the workload so that less time and energy is spent on things that can be handled through workflow automation. Once the upfront work of Grunt implementation has been completed, there is practically no additional work needed to run tasks. It is a very simple matter to create custom task runners for various build stages of projects with fine-grained control over what tasks get run for various stages. For instance, it is possible to create a custom task that includes error checking and syntax validation, running a suite of unit tests, and then, upon success, building the project to a development release version and generating a deployment archive. The possibilities for various build configurations are vast. However, first things first, there are some things that need to be discussed prior to diving in.

Dependencies

Before jumping into Grunt.js, you first need to understand that Grunt has some dependencies that are needed in order to get up and running with task automation. In this case, the dependencies are Node.js and Node Package Manager (NPM). While a deep level of Node.js knowledge is not a prerequisite to using Grunt.js, a high-level understanding of Node.js and NPM is needed to get started.

Node.js and NPM are required for the installation of the Grunt **command line interface** (CLI) as well as plugins that are used for task automation in Grunt. We will get into plugins later in the book, so don't be too concerned with what exactly a plugin is at this point. Suffice it to say that a plugin is a script that performs a certain task in Grunt. These tasks can be run individually or as a series of tasks that run as part of what is called a custom task. Some examples of common tasks are as follows:

- **JSHint**: JSHint runs JavaScript validation (lint). This runs code that analyzes JavaScript for errors or syntax that has the potential to be a bug.

- **Uglify**: This task minifies files by removing all excess characters from code without changing or breaking the functionality of the code.

- **LESS**: This is a task that compiles LESS files into CSS files.

- **Watch**: This responds to additions, changes, and deletions of files by running preconfigured tasks, for instance, if you wish to build your project or run lint on files every time the file is changed and saved.

An example usage scenario, using these tasks listed, might be to run JSHint to lint JavaScript source files. If errors exist, the task halts and provides message(s) related to the errors and warnings found. If no errors exist, then the task completes and the Uglify task is run to minify the JavaScript source files, outputting them to the distribution directory. Next, the LESS task is run to generate and output CSS to the distribution directory. Finally, the Watch task is run so that it will continue to monitor changes to files when they occur. Watch might start the entire build process again without any user interaction. This is really powerful and frees up the developer who would otherwise need to perform each task manually every time files were changed.

There are many official plugins such as these that have been created and are maintained by the Grunt team. Official plugins are prefixed with `contrib-`, so the naming of plugins listed previously would be found as `contrib-jshint`, `contrib-uglify`, `contrib-less`, and `contrib-watch` as each one of these plugins is officially maintained by the Grunt team.

There are unofficial plugins created and contributed to the project by other organizations and developers as well. Examples of common unofficial plugins include the following:

- **concurrent**: This runs tasks concurrently
- **newer**: This runs tasks on source files that have changed
- **open**: This opens URLs and files from a task
- **notify**: This provides automatic desktop notifications for errors and warnings

What has been listed here isn't even the tip of the iceberg of the plugins available to add to your project for workflow automation. You might find that you are spending time on a task that is repetitive and error prone. What if you could write a script that would perform this task for you and ensure that it is done correctly every time? Well, with Grunt, you can create your own plugins and even contribute them to the NPM registry so that others who have the same need can benefit.

Now that we have a bit of introduction of what Grunt can do, let's discuss more about the Node.js and NPM dependencies. In the following sections, we will get to know some introductory information about Node.js and NPM. We will look at procedures for the installation of Node, which will include upgrade processes as well as pristine installations on both Mac and Windows. The Grunt Command Line Interface will be introduced; this is where we will actually begin working with Grunt tooling:

- An overview of Node.js and NPM
- Upgrading or installing Node.js
- Using NPM to manage the Grunt CLI

Grunt.js and Grunt plugins require Node.js and NPM in order to be installed. As a result, Node.js and NPM are dependencies of Grunt. Node.js is the server environment in which Grunt will run. NPM is the package manager that will be used to install plugins from the NPM repository. NPM will make it easy to install code written by other developers who have shared their solutions so that others, such as us, can benefit from reuse.

In order to go further into details about Node.js and NPM, the following questions will be answered in this section:

- What is Node.js and NPM?
- Where can I find Node.js and NPM?

What is Node.js and NPM?

Node.js is a runtime environment that uses the Google V8 engine to execute JavaScript on your machine, be it OS X, Windows, Linux, or SunOS (at the time of writing). There are also some unofficial builds for other platforms provided by members of the community. If you use the Google Chrome web browser, then you are using an application built with the Google V8 engine. Google V8 implements ECMAScript and is an open source project. If you have not heard of ECMAScript prior to this book, ECMAScript is a language standards specification. Some well-known languages, which are varying degrees of implementation of ECMAScript, are JavaScript, Microsoft's jScript, and Adobe's ActionScript. By varying degrees, it is to be understood that a language such as JavaScript is not ECMAScript; rather, the JavaScript core implementation is based on ECMAScript, yet JavaScript implements features that are in addition to ECMAScript.

So, what is Node? The Node.js platform is an asynchronous event-driven framework, which allows developers to create network applications (for example, HTTP or SMTP). Node allows developers to create applications running on a host that can be accessed by clients on another host, for instance, a web browser accessing a website or an e-mail application requesting mail on a mail server. This is by no means the limit of the functionality of Node.js. Applications can be built to run on the Node.js environment, which do not require client/server architecture between separate hosts. In fact, Grunt.js is an example of an application that runs on Node.js within the same host environment. The Node.js environment makes it possible to write JavaScript programs that are not reliant on browser interpretation. Node.js allows developers to write JavaScript applications that run as server-side applications.

Node.js provides a package manager that we will use to install Grunt, aptly named **Node Package Manager** (**NPM**). NPM provides access to scripts and applications in the NPM registry along with the ability to manage these applications on the user's machine for installation and updates as well as some additional features such as publishing packages. Grunt and Grunt plugins require NPM to be installed because they are managed with NPM. A package manager is an application that provides a utility for developers to share and provide updates to their plugins, which, in turn, end users can use in order to install, configure, update, and remove these applications from their machines. NPM will provide you with just such a utility needed for Grunt and Grunt plugins. We will use NPM regularly to install and possibly update packages while we set up and configure Grunt in our application in order to provide task automation.

Where can I find Node.js and NPM?

Node.js is an open source project that is maintained by individuals who collaborate and help steer future development efforts of the platform:

All of the documentation and information about Node.js can be found on the Node.js organization website, https://www.nodejs.org/. Node.js isn't a brand new technology, yet it isn't that old either; Node.js' first release, v0.0.1, on GitHub was on May 27, 2009. Applications intended to run on the Node.js platform are written in JavaScript, allowing developers to leverage the expressiveness of JavaScript outside of the browser in a server-side environment.

NPM used to be a separately maintained project from Node.js, so in previous versions of Node.js, NPM was obtained through a separate installation. NPM is now provided as part of the Node.js core installation; when you install Node.js, you will have NPM without any further installation requirements. All that you will need to do is proceed to the downloads page on the Node.js site, https://nodejs.org/download/, choose the prebuilt installer for your platform, and download it on your machine. We will go over the upgraded and pristine installation of Node.js for both Mac and Windows in the next sections.

Upgrading or installing Node.js

In this section, we will go through the process of the Node.js installation. As of the time of writing this, the current version of Node.js is v4.3.1. Some readers may already be up and running with Node; for others, this may be the first introduction to the server platform. As a result, we will cover the steps necessary for both an upgrade and a new installation:

- Upgrading Node.js via NPM on Mac
- Upgrading Node.js via .msi and NPM
- The pristine installation of Node.js via a downloaded binary
- Adding your installation path to your $PATH variable

If you do not have Node.js installed on your machine, feel free to jump to the "Pristine Installation of Node.js via downloaded binary" section. If you have a previous version of Node installed, know that Grunt requires Node versions greater than or equal to 0.8.0. If you want to upgrade, it is strongly recommended that you perform a backup prior to performing the Node.js upgrade process. For those on Mac, continue reading the next section. For those of you on Windows, feel free to jump to the Upgrading Node.js via .msi and NPM section.

Upgrading Node.js via NPM on Mac

Upgrading Node.js via NPM is very straightforward and shows you just how great a utility NPM is. We will use a **Terminal** application in order to update Node from the command-line interface. This process assumes that you have an existing instance of Node.js installed globally. If you do not have Node.js installed as a global application, you will need to change directories to the location where Node.js is installed and perform the update from this location. A global installation of Node.js provides an entry to your PATH variable and you will be able to access it via the command line from any directory. A local installation might be in a project root where you are using specific Node.js versions in a project.

It is important to note that the upgrade process uses a Node binary manager module called n. The n module is not maintained by Node.js. Therefore, proceed with caution and at your own risk when performing the upgrade process that follows. Information on the n module can be found at its GitHub page, `https://github.com/tj/n`. It is strongly suggested that you review the project's documentation prior to proceeding with an upgrade. Additionally, make sure that you have a recent backup.

With this said, I have used the following upgrade process many times without the slightest issue. I am extremely confident in using the n module to upgrade my own Node.js versions.

To get started, first check for the current version of Node that is installed on your machine:

```
$ node --version
```

You can also use another command showed as follows:

```
$ node -v
```

This will display the currently installed version of node. Your result may differ but should look something like the following version, which was the output from calling the version command:

```
v0.10.29
```

The next line deletes the contents of the NPM cache so that we can ensure that we are not working with stale files/data. The `sudo` requests administrator privilege, `npm` defines the application to be used, `cache` manipulates the packages cache, and `clean` deletes the data from the cache directory. Depending on your user, you may need to include a super user prefix, such as `sudo`, in order to have permissions to perform the following commands. If you get an error message that alludes to permissions, then your user does not have sufficient privilege and the use of super user prefix or logging in as administrator user will be needed. Syntax using `sudo` is provided as it doesn't hurt anything to include it in the commands; however, it may not be necessary, depending on whether your installation exists globally or locally:

```
$ sudo npm cache clean -f
```

If you are using sudo and are not currently logged in as an administrator, you will be prompted for your password in the next line. If you are not using sudo, then this step will be omitted:

```
$ password:
```

Enter your password and press *ENTER* to continue.

You may now be presented with an NPM warning that notifies you that NPM is using force. This is seen because of the `-f` flag used in the command that was issued previously:

```
$ npm WARN using --force I sure hope you know what you are doing.
```

Continue with the installation. In the following line, I am using the `sudo` administrator to run the npm application in order to install the n application globally by using `-g`. I will use the n module to upgrade Node.js:

```
$ sudo npm install -g n
```

As n is installed, I will see some path information displayed, which shows where n has been installed. When this is complete, I am ready to upgrade node with the following command. The sudo administrator will use the n application to install the latest stable version of Node.js:

```
$ sudo n stable
```

The command runs n with the `stable` option. This will get the latest stable version of Node.js from the server. You can also request a specific version by replacing stable with the version string that you wish to install, for example, `sudo n 0.12.7`.

At this point, you should see a result similar to the following, which confirms the version being installed along with the path information. In this case, the result is that node-v0.12.7 was installed in a new directory located in `/usr/local/n/versions/node/0.12.7`. Confirmation of the installed version shows v0.12.7. Your version may differ significantly, so don't be alarmed by the version number represented here:

```
install : node-v0.12.7

        mkdir : /usr/local/n/versions/node/0.12.7

        fetch : https://nodejs.org/dist/v0.12.7/node-v0.12.7-darwin-x64.
tar.gz

    installed : v0.12.7
```

The entire Terminal series of commands should resemble the following screenshot. If, by chance, your node version was already up to date, n will not provide any output, as shown in the following screenshot:

```
drcsoft-mbp:~ dougrdotnet$ node --version
v0.10.29
drcsoft-mbp:~ dougrdotnet$ sudo npm cache clean -f
Password:
npm WARN using --force I sure hope you know what you are doing.
drcsoft-mbp:~ dougrdotnet$ sudo npm install -g n
/usr/local/bin/n -> /usr/local/lib/node_modules/n/bin/n
n@1.3.0 /usr/local/lib/node_modules/n
drcsoft-mbp:~ dougrdotnet$ sudo n stable

    install : node-v0.12.7
      mkdir : /usr/local/n/versions/node/0.12.7
      fetch : https://nodejs.org/dist/v0.12.7/node-v0.12.7-darwin-x64.tar.gz
  installed : v0.12.7
```

At this point, you have either successfully upgraded Node.js or discovered that your version of Node.js is up to date. In either case, you are now prepared to move forward to add your installation path to your $PATH variable.

Congratulations! You have updated Node.js.

Be sure to have a look at the n GitHub pages for other useful commands, such as 'rm' to remove Node.js. If you have multiple versions of Node.js installed, you can specify, similar to the installation, the version that you want to remove using the rm command.

Upgrading Node.js on Windows via .msi and NPM

For those of you that currently have Node installed on Windows, the process of upgrading is basically the same as that of a new installation. The simplest approach is to use the Node Windows Installer, .msi, available from the Node.js downloads page, `https://nodejs.org/download/`:

	Windows Installer node-v0.12.7-x86.msi	Macintosh Installer node-v0.12.7.pkg	Source Code node-v0.12.7.tar.gz
Windows Installer (.msi)	32-bit	64-bit	
Windows Binary (.exe)	32-bit	64-bit	
Mac OS X Installer (.pkg)	Universal		
Mac OS X Binaries (.tar.gz)	32-bit	64-bit	
Linux Binaries (.tar.gz)	32-bit	64-bit	
SunOS Binaries (.tar.gz)	32-bit	64-bit	
Source Code	node-v0.12.7.tar.gz		

Prior to beginning, check your current version of Node so that you can verify that you have successfully updated Node and NPM when the installation process was completed:

```
$ node -version
```

You can also use another command shown as follows:

```
$ node -v
```

Your expected output should be the version of Node that is currently installed on your machine:

```
v0.10.29
```

Choose the Windows Installer .msi file that is appropriate for your machine and download it. Once the download is completed, run the installer file to begin the Node.js installation. Follow the prompts to run the installation, accept the terms of the license agreement, and continue completing the installation.

The final step of the Windows upgrade process is to update all of the existing global packages. This will require cleaning of the package cache and then performing an update of all global packages. We can do this in two lines with the following commands:

```
npm cache clean
npm update -g
```

You have successfully upgraded Node.js or discovered that your version of Node.js is up to date. At this point, you are now prepared to move forward to add your installation path to your $PATH variable.

Congratulations, you have successfully updated Node.js!

The pristine installation of Node.js via downloaded binary

For those of you who do not have a version of Node.js installed yet, the following steps for the installation are for you. The examples illustrated here are from the Mac installer; while the Windows installer will be a little different, the installation process is basically the same. For this installation, we will download the binary installation file and install it on your machine. The current version as of the writing of this book is 4.3.1. Navigate to `https://nodejs.org/download/` to find the available downloads for various platforms:

	Windows Installer	Macintosh Installer	Source Code
	node-v0.12.7-x86.msi	node-v0.12.7.pkg	node-v0.12.7.tar.gz
Windows Installer (.msi)	32-bit		64-bit
Windows Binary (.exe)	32-bit		64-bit
Mac OS X Installer (.pkg)	Universal		
Mac OS X Binaries (.tar.gz)	32-bit		64-bit
Linux Binaries (.tar.gz)	32-bit		64-bit
SunOS Binaries (.tar.gz)	32-bit		64-bit
Source Code	node-v0.12.7.tar.gz		

Choose the correct download link for your platform. For the purposes of this book, we will use a binary installer (**.exe** for Windows or **.pkg** for Mac) and will not be building Node.js from source. The examples that follow will be for the Mac platform. If you are installing in Windows, simply follow the steps outlined in the installer application.

After downloading the binary, run the installer file to open the installation dialogue. The first view that we are presented with is the Introduction. Note the line defining the installation path. Click on **Continue** to proceed to review and accept the license agreement:

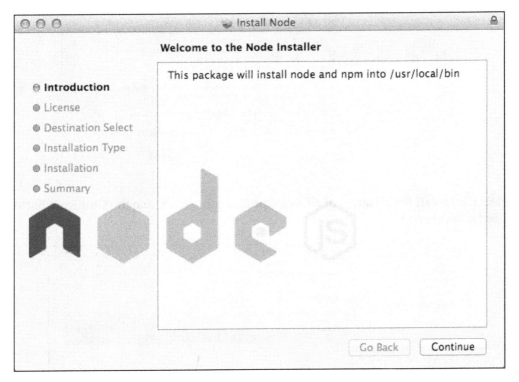

Click on **Continue**, and once you have reviewed the agreement, then **Agree** to the license that is presented in the pop-up window that is launched:

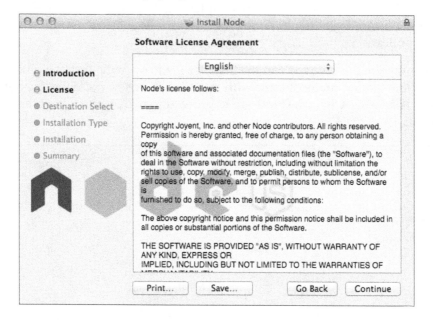

Select the **Install for all users of this computer** option to enable the **Continue** button in order to proceed:

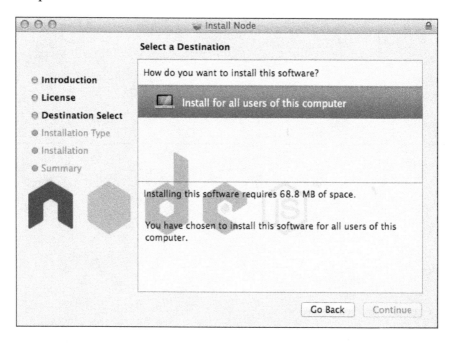

Press **Install** in order to accept the default location shown in step 1 of the installation:

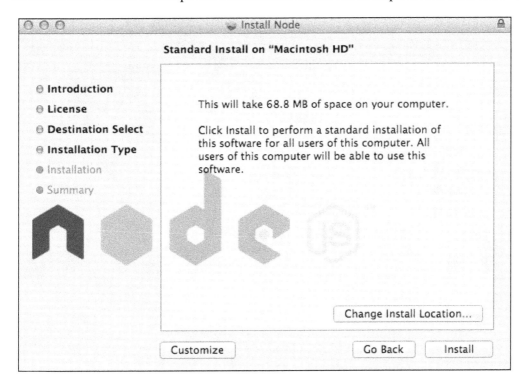

Node.js will be installed in the default, or specified, directory. You will then be presented with the summary view of the installation:

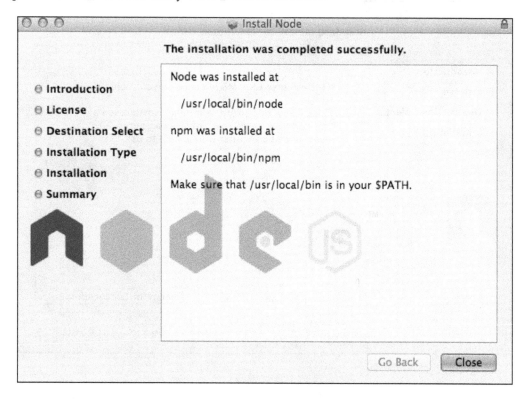

Congratulations, you have successfully updated Node.js!

Verify that your install location for node is on your path by checking for node's version from the Terminal command line:

```
$ node –version
```

If you receive an error resembling the following, then the installation path needs to be added to your $PATH variable:

```
-bash: node: command not found
```

The next section will cover how to add the installation path to your $PATH variable.

Adding your installation path to your $PATH variable

For Windows 7, the process of editing the Path variable is as follows:

1. Choose **Properties** from the **My Computer** context menu (right-click).
2. Choose the **Advanced** tab from the **System Properties** window.
3. Click on the **Environment Variables** button in the **Advanced** section of the window.
4. Select the **Path** item from the list of variables and click on the **Edit** button.
5. Append the path where node was installed to the Path variable; they are separated by semicolons.
6. Choose **OK** to save the changes to Path:

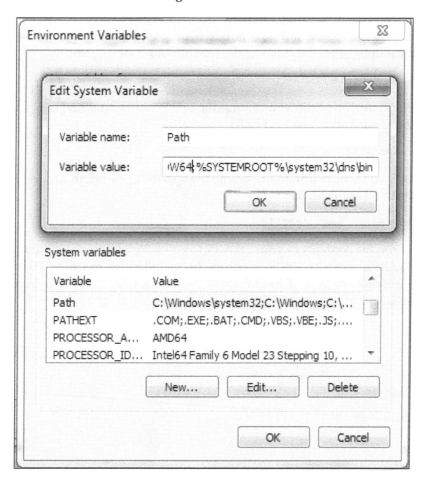

For Mac OS X, we will edit the $PATH variable from within **Terminal** using the **Nano editor**. You can use **vi editor** as well for the same purpose. It is even possible to use **Text Edit**.

To begin, let's first check our existing $PATH variable value by echoing the path variable in Terminal:

```
$ echo $PATH
```

You should see a result with the current value of your $PATH variable, the following for example:

```
$ /usr/bin:/bin:/usr/sbin:/sbin:/usr/local/bin
```

Next, change directories to the home directory using the **Change Directory (cd)** command:

```
$ cd
```

Create a .bash_profile file if it does not exist, or open the .bash_profile file in nano for the editing. This file exists at the root of your user directory:

```
$ nano .bash_profile
```

If you prefer to use Text Edit, you can use the open command with [-e], which instructs the command to use Text Edit:

```
open -e .bash_profile
```

You can use [-a] in the command to define the specific application to open the file by defining a named application:

```
open -a TextEdit .bash_profile
```

You should see the contents of your .bash_profile file in the nano editor. It will be empty if you have never created one before. In the following example, I have already defined locations to be included in my path. As you can see, my .bash_profile already exists and has content in it:

Add the following line to the file, where [PATH_TO_NODE_INSTALL_DIRECTORY] is the path where the Node installer application installed Node.js:

```
PATH=$PATH:[PATH_TO_NODE_INSTALL_DIRECTORY]
```

Save the file in nano by pressing *Ctrl + O* and confirm that the filename is to be saved as `.bash_profile` by hitting return. Exit nano by pressing *Ctrl + X*.

You can exit **terminal** and reopen in order to start a new terminal session and allow the changes to take effect; however, an even better way is to enter the following command to reload your `.bash_profile`:

```
$ source .bash_profile
```

In this method, there is no need to restart the Terminal application; the source command executes the file defined as the argument — in this case, .bash_profile — thus the $PATH variable has been updated.

Using NPM to install the Grunt Command Line Interface

Up until this point, we have been working on installing the dependencies of Grunt. Now, we finally get to start working on the installation of the Grunt CLI. Installing the Grunt CLI is the first step in the process of setting up automated tasks with Grunt and we will use the CLI for all of our grunt work. While this was a pun and not that funny, the CLI has one specific purpose: to be able to run the `grunt` command from anywhere on your system. This is why we will be installing the CLI globally, which means that it will be able to run from any location, globally, on your machine.

Installing the Grunt CLI

NPM is used to install Grunt and the Grunt CLI. The process of installation is very simple. As we just completed the updating or installing of Node, it should not be necessary to update NPM. If it has been a while since you updated NPM, now would be a good time to do so. Updating NPM is very simple and straightforward.

Updating NPM

Updating NPM is performed in one line. We will use the [`sudo`] administrator to run the [`npm`] application in order to [`update`] the [`npm`] application globally [`-g`]:

```
sudo npm update -g npm
```

That's right! We use NPM to update itself! The `sudo npm` command specifies that we want to run NPM as an administrator, the `-g` flag denotes a global update, and the ensuing `npm` specifies that NPM is the application that we are updating. This is the basic syntax for all NPM commands.

Installing Grunt CLI

The Grunt CLI is the first thing that we need to install as the Grunt CLI's sole responsibility is to run Grunt, as mentioned in the previous section. When we issue the install command, we will be placing the grunt command to the global path so that it is available from within all of your projects. Acting as the [`sudo`] administrator, we will run [`npm`] in order to [`install`] the [`grunt-cli`] globally [`-g`]:

```
sudo npm install -g grunt-cli
```

It is important to point out that we are not installing Grunt at this point. As mentioned, the primary purpose of the CLI is to run Grunt. Perhaps this sounds a bit confusing at the moment, but don't overthink it. What this means is that we will be installing Grunt within each project using the Grunt CLI. As a result, this will provide a means for us to maintain control over Grunt versions associated with projects. For example, say the current version of Grunt at the time you started a project was v0.4.3. You would be able to install this Grunt version in your project without affecting any other project-specific implementation of Grunt. Later, in case you begin a new project and the current version is v0.4.5, you will be able to install this version in your new project without affecting the project with v0.4.3 implemented. If you wish, you could update your first project from v0.4.3 to v0.4.5. This results in your ability to upgrade Grunt within a project as you see fit without affecting any instance of Grunt being used for other projects. When you run Grunt from the CLI, it will be associated with a local version of a Grunt configuration file, known as a **gruntfile**. Grunt can be run from any directory in your project.

If you try to run Grunt from outside of your project directory, in a location where Grunt has not been installed with the Grunt CLI, you will receive an error such as the following:

```
grunt-cli: The grunt command line interface. (v0.1.13)
Fatal error: Unable to find local grunt.
```

If you're seeing this message, either a Gruntfile wasn't found or Grunt hasn't been installed locally to your project. For more information about installing and configuring Grunt, please see the Getting Started guide:

```
http://gruntjs.com/getting-started
```

In this case, you will need to either install Grunt in the location that you expected it to be or change directories to the location where Grunt is actually installed.

Summary

Grunt is a JavaScript task runner whose purpose is task automation. Using automation, developers can find benefits through improved productivity, error reduction, and reduced workload of mundane tasks. You learned that Grunt has some dependencies that need to be installed before we can begin using Grunt in our projects. Grunt requires that Node.js and the NPM be installed so that we can install the Grunt CLI, which we will use to install Grunt. It wasn't necessary to get too deep into the understanding of Node.js and NPM at this point; we only needed to have a high-level understanding of the technologies in order to help us get the Grunt CLI up and running.

Some plugins were mentioned, such as contrib-watch, contrib-jshint, and contrib-uglify, that will be used later to illustrate task configuration to automate our workflows. As you perform your daily development activities, perhaps you can identify the repetition of certain tasks. Imagine being able to automate these tasks; with Grunt, you could write your own plugin to do just this. You could even share it with others by contributing it as an unofficial Grunt plugin.

The next chapter will cover the creation of an application that will be used for examples throughout the remainder of this book. This will involve using an application scaffold, which will generate an AngularJS application. This will allow the rapid setting up of the environment needed to write, build, and run the Grunt automated tasks that will be covered in later chapters.

2
Foundation for Creating an App using Angular.JS

Now that we have had an introduction to Grunt, and Grunt dependencies, in *Chapter 1*, *Grunt Dependencies* we can move forward and look at how we can set up a project scaffold and be ready to begin development. While this chapter deals with the creation of an Angular.JS application, your project does not have to be an Angular application in order to use Grunt. We are simply using Angular as an example as it is such a popular frontend framework. As such, we won't get too deep into Angular.JS since the scope of information is broad enough that we could write an entirely separate book. It should also be noted that Grunt exists as the build system used in a project called Yeoman. Yeoman combines scaffolding (yo), build systems (Grunt), and a package manager, for example, for a complete application generator solution. As we are focused on Grunt, we will not be using Yeoman in the following examples. Be sure to check out Yeoman at `http://yeoman.io/`, however, as it does provide a full suite of functionality.

There are a few things that we will have a look at in this chapter. We will be using Git, which is what is known as a distributed version control system. Distributed version control describes a peer-to-peer system of managing code repositories. What this means is that each user of the system has their own local clone of the code repository. This differs from a centralized version control system in that a single central repository exists on a server in which clients must check out and commit changes but they do not have the entire repository history stored locally.

Some readers may be familiar with version control systems such as **Subversion (SVN)** or CVS. Like SVN and CVS, Git is a version control system that can be used locally, for your own small projects, or for enterprise-level applications. Using any version control system is better than no system of managing versions at all. It is my opinion that version control should be used for any software application project, regardless of whether you are writing for yourself or a client. The benefits of version control are worth the small bit of effort needed in order to install a version control system.

Git happens to be very simple to install, with a few potential roadblocks to overcome. For the purposes of this book, we will be using a small subset of Git commands in order to accomplish some tasks; learning Git is beyond the scope of this book. GitHub has a great resource to learn Git, which can be found at `https://try.github.io/levels/1/challenges/1`. More information on Git can be found on the Git website: `http://git-scm.com/`.

We will use Git as a means to install the Angular Seed Project. This is a project that creates an Angular project scaffold (skeleton) for us automatically using Node.js and NPM. Angular Seed will set us up with an example project that we can use to get started quickly without the need to manually create all of the project files and directory tree. This will help us keep the setting up to a simple process and provide a starting point for an app that can be modified to suit individual needs:

- Installing Git
- Creating the Angular Seed Project
- Installation summary for more advanced users

Installing Git

Git is a distributed version control system that allows developers to manage changes to files. Git provides you with a means to store application versions so that we can track changes as backups and share updates within teams and with users. We will be using Git in this chapter in order to install an application called Angular Seed. Angular Seed will create an application scaffold for us so that we can quickly create our starting application files and directories automatically. As we are really interested in automating processes, including Angular Seed makes sense to get us going quickly. It should be noted that there used to be a Grunt plugin project named grunt-angular-seed. However, it is no longer maintained and has been deprecated. As a result, we will simply use Git to clone the Angular Seed project in our project's root directory. At that point, we will be able to go through the simple installation process for Angular Seed.

Determining the Git installation

On Mac, if you have Xcode installed, you will be using the Xcode command-line developer tools. If you do not already have git installed, or if it is installed but you have uninstalled Xcode since installing Git, you will receive an error that Xcode is required in order to run the `git` command. Proceed with the following process to check for an existing installation and make the following modifications if necessary:

```
git --version
```

If you have git installed already, you should get an output similar to the following:

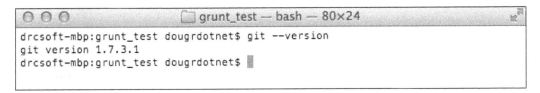

If you mistype `git` or Git is not installed, you will get the following error:

```
-bash: get: command not found
drcsoft-mbp:grunt_test dougrdotnet$ 
```

If Xcode cannot find the Git installation or Xcode was previously installed and then uninstalled, you may see the following error message:

```
xcode-select: note: no developer tools were found at '/Applications/Xcode.app',
requesting install. Choose an option in the dialog to download the command line
developer tools.
```

If this is the case, you will be prompted to install Xcode and/or the command-line developer tools with the following popup:

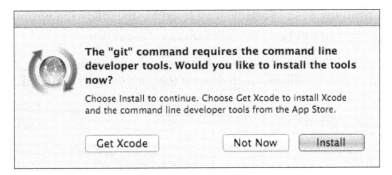

If you wish to install Xcode, then proceed by clicking on **Get Xcode**. It is, however, not necessary to install Xcode. You can install only the command-line tools by clicking on **Install** and proceeding through the installation process. Another option to use Git and not install Xcode is to create an alias to your Git install location. If you do not have Git installed yet and you receive this popup after going through the installation process that we will cover shortly, come back to this section to refer to creating aliases to your Git installation.

Creating a temporary alias

To add a temporary alias we need to write the following command:

```
alias git="/usr/local/git/bin/git"
```

The alias command maps the shortcut `git` to the `"/usr/local/git/bin/git"` path, which is the default installation location of Git. You can then use the `git` command from any location on your system for the remainder of your Terminal session.

While this is useful, in this case, it is probably not exactly what you want. You can use Git often for many years to come through many different terminal sessions. You may recall from *Adding your installation path to your $PATH variable* section from *Chapter 1*, *Grunt Dependencies* we stepped through the process of adding the installation path of Node to your $PATH variable. We need to do the same for git in order to make a permanent alias. Let's walk through the process again using the path required for Git.

Adding Git to your $PATH variable

As we did previously, we will edit the $PATH variable using the Nano editor from within Terminal.

1. Check your existing $PATH variable value:

   ```
   $ echo $PATH
   ```

2. Your resulting $PATH variable may resemble the following terminal output:

   ```
   $ /usr/bin:/bin:/usr/sbin:/sbin:/usr/local/bin
   ```

3. Change directories to the home directory, which is where .bash_profile already exists or will be created (cd is the command to change directories):

   ```
   $ cd
   ```

4. If it does not exist, `.bash_profile` file will be created. If it does exist, `.bash_profile` will be edited. Simply enter the following in **Terminal** to create or open the file to edit:

```
$ nano .bash_profile
```

The contents of your `.bash_profile` file should appear in the Nano editor. If the file is empty, then you are in the process of creating a new file. If there is content in the file, then you already have an existing `.bash_profile`. In the following example, note that git has already been added to my path (`PATH = $PATH:/usr/local/git/bin/`).

1. Add the path location for Git to your `.bash_profile` file:

2. Save the file in nano by pressing *Ctrl + O* and confirm the filename to be saved as `.bash_profile` by hitting return. Exit nano by pressing *Ctrl + X*. Remember to restart terminal or enter the following command to reload your `.bash_profile`:

```
$ source .bash_profile
```

3. Note that you can also add the alias to your `.bash_profile` using the same syntax that was used to create the temporary one. So, instead of adding to your path variable as described previously, simply add the following to your `.bash_profile`:

```
alias git="/usr/local/git/bin/git"
```

Installation of Git

If Git is not installed on your system, then the easiest way to get Git is from the Git website:

```
http://git-scm.com/
```

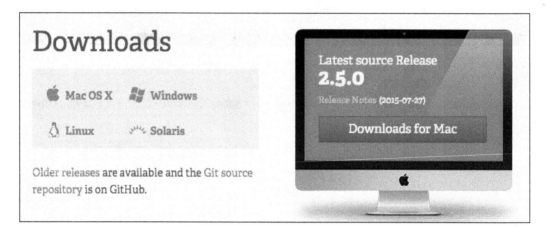

Navigate to the Git downloads page, `http://git-scm.com/downloads`, and choose the correct installer for your system.

Be sure to follow the installation instructions provided in `README.txt` that is included with the installer download for your platform. We will outline the install process using the Mac package installer.Once downloaded, run the installer image file (.dmg) that you downloaded.

This will open the image in Finder where you can access the installation files. Be sure to review README.txt before proceeding. You should see the following in the Finder window that opens when running the installation image. Double-click on the git-2.4.3-universal-mavericks.pkg file in order to run the package installer:

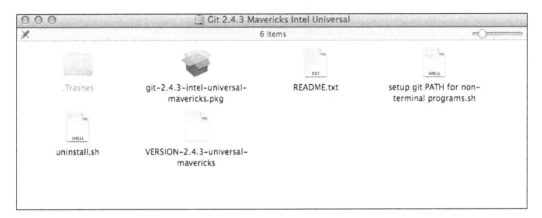

Depending upon your security preferences for the installation of applications outside the Mac App Store, your installation may not be allowed and you will see the following pop-up message:

If this is the case, it will be necessary to override your security settings for this installation from **System Preferences**. Open **Security and Privacy** preferences to allow the installation. Choose **Open Anyway** in order to allow the installer to run:

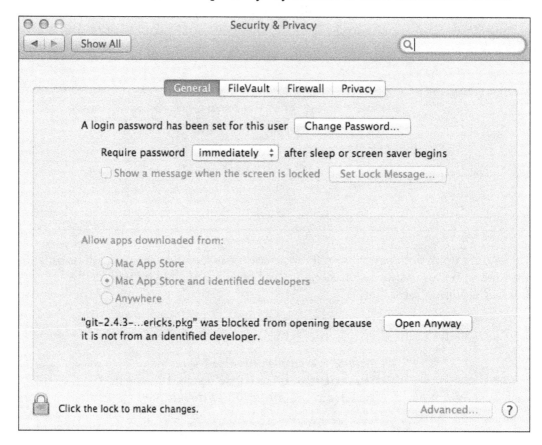

You will now be presented with the installation dialog:

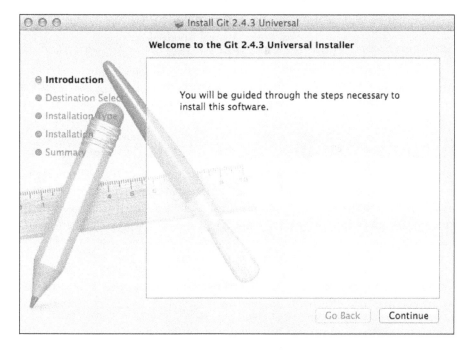

Follow the step-by-step installation as guided by the dialog in order to install Git.

Congratulations, you have installed git!

Creating the Angular Seed Project

Now that we have installed Git, we can check out the Angular Seed Project from its GitHub repository. The project is located at `https://github.com/angular/angular-seed`. Angular Seed is an application that will generate an Angular.JS project scaffold, also known as a skeleton. The generated application skeleton is a simple project that includes a couple of views and controllers that provide examples of how to use the Angular framework. Angular Seed also creates some ready-to-run unit tests. We won't get into the topic of unit testing here as we simply wish to scaffold an example project that we can then use to illustrate Grunt with. For more information on unit testing configured with Angular Seed, see the project unit testing section at `https://github.com/angular/angular-seed#running-unit-tests`.

Dependencies of Angular Seed

The only Angular Seed dependencies are Git and Node.js (along with NPM). In *Chapter 1*, *Grunt Dependencies* we went through the installation of Node.js in detail. If you have not yet installed Node.js or are unsure, refer to *Chapter 1*, *Grunt Dependencies* to make sure that you have the necessary dependencies installed and configured for your system. Not only do we need Node.js for Angular Seed, but we also need it for the remainder of this book's primary topic, Grunt.

Cloning the Angular Seed Project

The first task that we need to complete is to create our project root directory. Given that the example will be a web application, I suggest creating the project root in the location where you manage your web project directories. For this project, I will create a sample_project root directory in my `4875_CH2_Project` folder. You can name your project directory anything you like. Note that, when you clone the Angular Seed project, you will create a new directory in the process.

Once we have created the project root directory, we need to open a Terminal window and change directories to the new location.

Your paths may differ so simply change the paths in the following examples to the location where your root directory is located.

Note that, in both Windows and Mac, it is possible to drag a folder to the command prompt or Terminal and have it complete the path for you so that you do not need to type the entire path:

`cd /path/to/your/project/directory/`

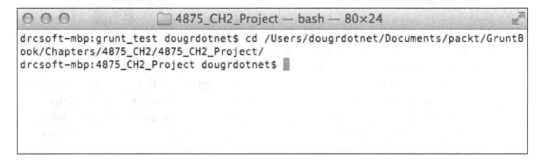

Now that we are inside the directory that we wish to clone the Angular Seed project to, we will use Git to clone the directory from its repository location to the current directory.

When you clone a project with Git, you will get all of the project history along with it as Git is a version control system. For our needs, we do not need all of the history so we will specify that we only want a depth of one revision. It is perfectly fine to get all of the history but it won't be necessary as we aren't working on the Angular Seed project itself; we are only using it for the scaffolding of our custom project. In order to clone the project with only the latest revision of the branch that we are cloning, we will use the following Git command syntax. Be sure to change [Your Project Name] to the name of your project:

```
git clone --depth=1 https://github.com/angular/angular-seed.git [Your
Project Name]
```

- In my example, I created a project named sample_project in my project directory using the following syntax:

  ```
  git clone --depth=1 https://github.com/angular/angular-seed.git
  sample_project
  ```

- At this point, you will have the Angular Seed project cloned and ready to finish setting up:

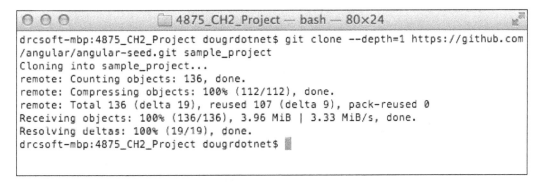

You should now have a project tree which looks as follows:

Installing Angular Seed dependencies

Before we can run our sample application, we need to complete the installation of dependencies for Angular Seed. We will use npm to install our dependencies. From our new project directory, we simply need to run the npm install command. When we run npm install, we will get two things: tools that are needed by Angular Seed and the actual Angular code that is obtained though another package manager automatically. The other package manager is **Bower**. Like NPM, Bower manages packages. As we are using NPM, we will not address Bower further. Suffice it to say that the Angular-Seed project requires it; therefore, you will see Bower in your project tree. NPM is designed to manage Node packages where Bower's purpose is to manage frontend JavaScript packages. We will get the developer tools needed via NPM and the Angular code from Bower; we will get both with one single command.

1. First, let's change directories to our new project folder, where [Your Project Directory] is the name of your directory:

   cd [Your Project Directory]

2. I changed directories to sample_project, which is the name of my project directory:

```
⬤ ⬤ ⬤                    🗀 sample_project — bash — 80×24
drcsoft-mbp:4875_CH2_Project dougrdotnet$ cd sample_project/
drcsoft-mbp:sample_project dougrdotnet$ ▉
```

If you have any confusion as to what directory you should be in at this time, know that the npm install command will be looking for a package.json file. If you refer back to the *Cloning the Angular Seed Project* section, you will see that the package.json file resides directly under my project folder named sample_project. If you are not in the correct location to run npm install, then you will receive an error as follows:

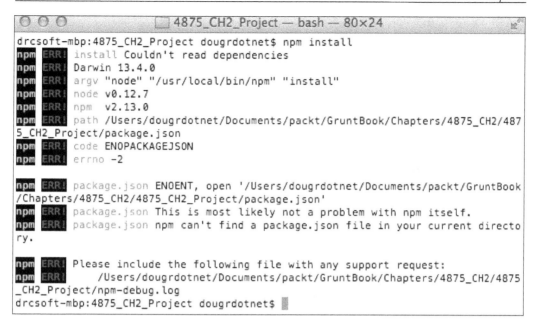

```
drcsoft-mbp:4875_CH2_Project dougrdotnet$ npm install
npm ERR! install Couldn't read dependencies
npm ERR! Darwin 13.4.0
npm ERR! argv "node" "/usr/local/bin/npm" "install"
npm ERR! node v0.12.7
npm ERR! npm  v2.13.0
npm ERR! path /Users/dougrdotnet/Documents/packt/GruntBook/Chapters/4875_CH2/487
5_CH2_Project/package.json
npm ERR! code ENOPACKAGEJSON
npm ERR! errno -2

npm ERR! package.json ENOENT, open '/Users/dougrdotnet/Documents/packt/GruntBook
/Chapters/4875_CH2/4875_CH2_Project/package.json'
npm ERR! package.json This is most likely not a problem with npm itself.
npm ERR! package.json npm can't find a package.json file in your current directo
ry.

npm ERR! Please include the following file with any support request:
npm ERR!     /Users/dougrdotnet/Documents/packt/GruntBook/Chapters/4875_CH2/4875
_CH2_Project/npm-debug.log
drcsoft-mbp:4875_CH2_Project dougrdotnet$
```

You will also find a new error log file in the location where you attempted to run the npm install command, named npm-debug.log. This log file is an output of the error; review the file and feel free to discard when you have completed the review.

Once you are in the correct location, you can complete the Angular Seed installation with the following command:

```
npm install
```

Is this your reaction? *Whoa! I ran into problems here!* If so, continue reading; we will get it sorted out.

At this point, if on Mac, it is possible that you might receive an error like we described earlier, related to Xcode and no developer tools found. This can occur because Bower is using Git to install the Angular code and is not mapping Git on our path as we wish. It is possible to install the Xcode developer tools without installing Xcode. Apple has made these separate packages.

1. We can install the developer tools by issuing the following command:
    ```
    xcode-select -install
    ```

2. Your output should look similar to the following:

```
drcsoft-mbp:sample_project dougrdotnet$ xcode-select --install
xcode-select: note: install requested for command line developer tools
drcsoft-mbp:sample_project dougrdotnet$
```

3. You will then be presented with a popup to install the Xcode developer tools. Click on **Install** to begin the installation:

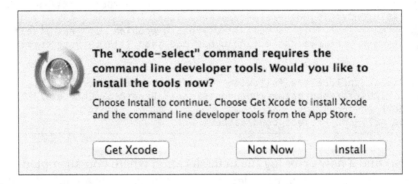

4. Click on **Agree** in the license agreement in the next window and complete the installation.

Alternatively, if you run into problems trying to install only the developer tools via the command line, you can visit https://developer.apple.com/downloads/ and obtain the developer tools installer for your operating system version:

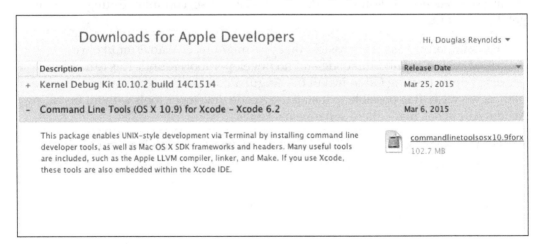

I am going to describe the download installer process as I am not on the most recent version of OS X and need to install via the download. I downloaded the .dmg image file from the developer downloads shown previously.

1. Double-clicking on the installer opens up a window with the Command Line Tools package installer:

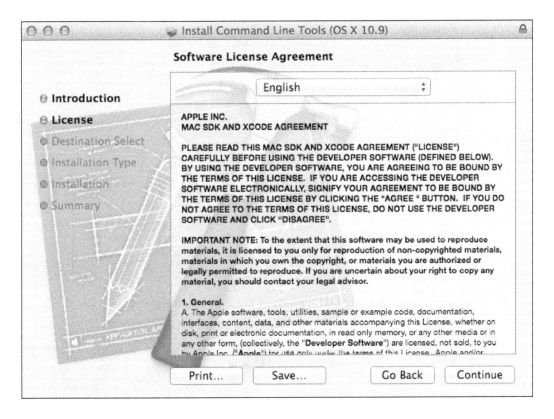

2. In the next step, note the size of the installation and accept the default installation location by clicking on **Install**: (You may need to enter your username and password to allow the installation.)

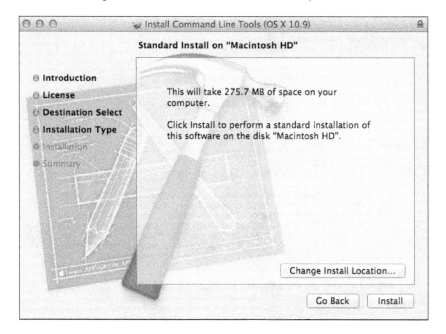

3. This will complete your installation of the Apple Developer Command Line Tools:

Now we can get back to installing the Angular Seed dependencies. If you had to go through all of the Command Line Tools installation, then you are back at running the npm install command from within your project folder.

So let's run the install command:

npm install

You should get a series of Terminal output related to the Bower installation of all the Angular code needed for the sample application:

Congratulations! You have installed the Angular Seed application!

Running the Angular Seed Application

We are now ready to run our sample application to ensure that everything has been installed correctly. One of the beautiful things about Node is that it is possible to create a locally running HTTP server without the need for a server application such as Apache, or having to use IIS on Windows. With Node, a server can be created easily and used to run and test your web applications in your browser.

- The Angular Seed application has a preconfigured server ready for us; all we need to do is start the server with this command:

  `npm start`

  This will create a running server.

- Verify that you have a similar output as shown here:

```
●  ●  ○                   sample_project — node — 80×58
drcsoft-mbp:sample_project dougrdotnet$ npm start

> angular-seed@0.0.0 prestart /Users/dougrdotnet/Documents/packt/GruntBook/Chapt
ers/4875_CH2/4875_CH2_Project/sample_project
> npm install


> angular-seed@0.0.0 postinstall /Users/dougrdotnet/Documents/packt/GruntBook/Ch
apters/4875_CH2/4875_CH2_Project/sample_project
> bower install


> angular-seed@0.0.0 start /Users/dougrdotnet/Documents/packt/GruntBook/Chapters
/4875_CH2/4875_CH2_Project/sample_project
> http-server -a localhost -p 8000 -c-1

Starting up http-server, serving ./ on port: 8000
Hit CTRL-C to stop the server
```

You can see in the output that an HTTP server was created at localhost using port 8000. This means that you can browse to localhost with this port assignment to launch the sample application.

- Open your browser and enter (or click on this URL if you are reading this as an e-book) `http://localhost:8000/app/index.html`. You will be presented with the Angular Seed skeleton web application:

Now we have a running web application with a couple of views that are wired to controllers and navigable by the links at the top of the application page. We will be able to use this application as our base to learn how to add Grunt automated tasks. You will learn more about tasks in the upcoming chapter.

- In order to stop the server, hit *Ctrl + C* in Terminal:

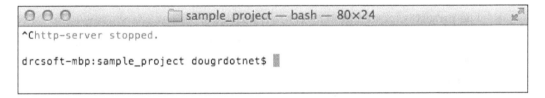

You can also quit the running Terminal/command prompt application and the server will be stopped.

Congratulations! You have successfully installed the Angular Seed application!

Installation summary – a quick guide

We will be installing the Angular Seed project using Git.

Installing Git

We will use this project throughout the book as our sample project. It is good to periodically check your current git version and current release notes for a new version to determine if upgrading is appropriate. Refer to `https://git-scm.com/` for the most current Git information.

If you wish to review any of the installation processes for Git, refer to the previous sections for specific installation or troubleshooting steps:

Determining Git Installation

Let's understand the use of Git for installation of Xcode on Mac systems:

- Adding Git to Your $PATH variable:
    - For example: `PATH = $PATH:/usr/local/git/bin/`
- If Git is not installed:
    - Installation of Git - `http://git-scm.com/`

In this chapter and for the remainder of the book, we will be using the Angular Seed project. The main reason for this is that it is simple to use the scaffold in order to set up a quick project with an HTTP server.

Create the Angular Seed Project

Checkout the Angular Seed Project from its Github repository

- The project is located at `https://github.com/angular/angular-seed`.
- Angular Seed is an application that will generate an Angular.js project scaffold.
- Dependencies of Angular Seed.
- Git and Node.js are the only dependencies of Angular Seed (See *Chapter 1, Grunt Dependencies*, for information regarding installation of Node.js).
- Clone the Angular Seed Project.
- `cd` into your project root and clone Angular Seed.

    ```
    git clone --depth=1 https://github.com/angular/angular-seed.git
    sample_project
    ```

- Installation of the Angular Seed Project dependencies.
- Run npm install from within the sample project that was just created. This will install all of the files required by the project scaffold and Bower will manage installation of all the Angular code needed by the sample application.

- In order to run the Angular Seed application, simply run the following command to launch an HTTP server running on port `8000`:

  `npm start`

- Open the application by navigating to `http://localhost:8000/app/index.html`. Stop the running server with *Ctrl + C*.

Summary

We really accomplished quite a bit in this chapter. We were able to lay the groundwork to work with Grunt by creating a sample application. After all, we need a project to automate. At this time, it is not necessary for us to be spending time trying to figure out what application we want to build and how we are going to approach it. Rather, we can use an application like Angular Seed to generate our application skeleton for us. Now that you have been introduced to this scaffolding tool, you will be able to use it for any future Angular.JS applications you need to bootstrap.

We covered the installation of Git as it was used for the cloning of Angular Seed and also used in the setup and configuration of an Angular Seed sample application by installing its dependencies. As you learned, there can be some roadblocks that can prevent us from easily installing tools from the command line. We covered a few ways to get the command-line tools up and running, depending on different problems that you might have run into along the way.

Once we were able to get past any command-line tool issues, we were able to run the npm install command from within our project so that the Angular Seed dependencies would be resolved. Once this was done, we were able to launch a local HTTP server instance easily and then navigate to it to ensure that our application was running as we expected. Now, whenever we want to test our changes, we can navigate to our application's URL to check and make sure that our modifications are looking and behaving as we expect.

In the next chapter, we will take a look at Grunt plugins. Plugins, or tasks, are the work-horses of Grunt task automation. You will learn to identify tasks that will be of benefit to you in your projects. Through this identification, you will discern the information that you need in order to find plugins that will provide solutions to the problems that you want to solve. We will, by example, go through the process of installation and configuration of plugins and how they are implemented in your project.

3
All about Grunt Plugins

Grunt plugins are core to Grunt functionality and, thus, are an important aspect of Grunt because plugins are what we use in order to design an automated build process. A plugin is a task. I may refer to plugins as tasks as you continue through the book, so consider plugins and tasks to be synonymous. Generally speaking, I may use the term **Task** when referring to plugins in terms of the specific work that they perform. A task is a unit of work that must be performed in order to accomplish a desired outcome, usually, as a portion of work that must be done in order to complete a larger process; although, a task may be in and of itself a standalone process. We may not know, offhand, exactly what tasks are needed to perform on a project. Grunt is scalable in this way, and it is easy to add tasks as we are working through our project. If you have done a few projects, then you will have a good idea for some tasks that you might like to automate. Perhaps, you run lint from a keyboard shortcut after each time you save changes to your code. Maybe you use some plugins in your editor that minify your CSS for you. Often, we will want to build our source code in our compiled source deployment files, and it is necessary to manually build our source each time we save our project to test. In web projects, we have to continually refresh our browser as we make changes so that we can see the latest updates that we have made. These, and many more tasks, are the candidates that we may choose to automate with Grunt. The aim of this chapter is to introduce you to some of these common tasks so that you will become aware of what types of tasks are already available, where to find them, and details of what these tasks will do for you:

- Obtaining Grunt plugins
- Discussing common Grunt plugins and their purposes

Obtaining Grunt plugins

The first step in getting started with Grunt plugins is to establish some fundamental understanding of which plugins are available, how they are installed, and how you actually use them in your workflow. It is important to begin considering what your project's needs are and what you wish to be able to turn over to automation, rather than manually completing yourself. Perhaps, you don't know the answers to these questions at this time, and that is fine. We will hopefully prompt you to begin asking yourself these questions and researching for answers. Obviously, that is why you are reading this book; you understand that task automation can benefit you and your development process. Let's get an idea of what is out there and how you can learn more.

Plugins overview

The available Grunt plugins are listed on the Grunt plugins page, located at: `http://gruntjs.com/plugins`. From this page, you can find a list of available plugins that is updated automatically. As this list is fetched dynamically from the NPM module database, you will always be able to view the most updated list of Grunt plugins from this page. As of the time of writing this, officially maintained plugins are prefixed with `contrib-` and have the image of a star next to them:

Plugin	Updated	Grunt Version	Downloads last 30 days
contrib-watch by Grunt Team — Run predefined tasks whenever watched file patterns are added, changed or deleted.	about a year ago	~0.4.0	766286
contrib-clean by Grunt Team — Clean files and folders.	about a year ago	~0.4.0	766132
contrib-uglify by Grunt Team — Minify files with UglifyJS.	6 months ago	>=0.4.0	751418
contrib-jshint by Grunt Team — Validate files with JSHint.	7 months ago	~0.4.5	750938

Other plugins found here are maintained by community contributors and not the Grunt team. They will not include the `contrib-` prefix, nor will they be marked with a star:

mocha-test by Peter Halliday A grunt task for running server side mocha tests	7 months ago		113410
sass by Sindre Sorhus Compile Sass to CSS using node-sass	5 months ago		102632
wiredep by Stephen Sawchuk Inject your Bower dependencies right into your HTML from Grunt.	9 months ago	~0.4.0	90468
rev by Sebastiaan Deckers Static file asset revisioning through content hashing	2 years ago		84156

Now would be a good time to navigate through the plugins' pages and get an idea of the types of tasks that are already available for you to use in your projects. Becoming even a little familiar with what is already there will help when you want to find a solution for a specific task.

Be sure to drill into any tasks you are interested in finding more information on. Each plugin has its own page and provides documentation about the plugin. In the next section, some of these common tasks will be chosen and described in more detail.

Actually obtaining Grunt plugins

It is important to note that we do not actually obtain plugins from the Grunt plugins page; this is merely where we can find available plugins and their associated documentation. Grunt plugins are installed using NPM. For example, in order to install a plugin in our project, we would navigate to our project's directory and use the `npm install` command for the plugin:

```
npm install [package name] -save-dev
```

Let's break this line down. We are running the `npm install` command to invoke NPM to install a package, `[package name]`. Then, we are issuing an optional -save-dev flag that instructs `npm` to save the package locally to your devDependencies located in the package.json file.

More discussion is needed on the usage of the optional flags for the install command. At this time we have not yet discussed the package.json file in detail, other than it was created for us in the Angular-Seed project setup. There are a couple ways to create a package.json file. When we use a command called grunt init to install most templates, a package.json file will be created for us. When we use the npm init command, a package.json file will be created. You can also create one manually and add it to your project. You can find documentation on creating your own package. json file at `http://gruntjs.com/getting-started#package.json`.

We will be using the package.json file that was automatically generated for us. Navigate to the Angular Seed project that we created in the last project. In this, you will find a file named package.json at the root of the project. Open this file with any text editor so that we can inspect the file. Find the section of the file that looks like the following:

```
"devDependencies": {
    "bower": "^1.3.1",
    "http-server": "^0.6.1",
    "jasmine-core": "^2.3.4",
    "karma": "~0.12",
    "karma-chrome-launcher": "^0.1.12",
    "karma-firefox-launcher": "^0.1.6",
    "karma-jasmine": "^0.3.5",
    "karma-junit-reporter": "^0.2.2",
    "protractor": "^2.1.0",
    "shelljs": "^0.2.6"
},
```

Notice the `devDependencies` key. In this json object are all of the key-value pairs that define the installed packages in our sample_project application. There are other objects that define dependency types, such as dependencies and optionalDependencies. These additional options will be discussed shortly. Recall that Angular-Seed required Bower and needed to create an HTTP server. Those dependencies were installed for us in the project setup process. When you use the `--save-dev` flag in the install command, you are instructing NPM to register the package in the `devDependencies` object of your package.json file. If devDependencies does not exist, then it will be created. Some other notable flags are as follows:

`npm install [package name] --save`

The `--save` flag creates, if it does not exist, or adds a section named dependencies:

`npm install [package name] --save-optional`

The `--save-optional` flag will create or add a section named optionalDependencies.

As we will be working with the sample_project development dependencies, and not the sample_project itself, we will be using `--save-dev`.

When plugins are installed, an entry will be made in package.json. Depending upon which save option is used, in which section the entry will be created will be determined. Additionally, when each plugin is installed, the related plugin files will be added to a directory named node-modules. This directory will be located at the root of the project folder. All plugins that will be used in sample_project will be configured in a file named Gruntfile.js. This is the main configuration file used by Grunt.js for workflow automation.

It should be noted that plugins can be run manually by issuing the 'grunt [plugin-name]' command. The manual command for each plugin will be listed in each task described later in the chapter where relevant.

For now, this is enough discussion of package.json. We will be looking at package. json in more detail as we progress through the book. Let's move on and take a look at some specific plugins in an effort to become more familiar with what types of tasks are available and get a better feel for what is needed in our project. As you become more experienced in using Grunt for task automation, you will probably find that you have a core set of plugins that are used in mostly all of your projects. Learning what these tasks are is your first step in creating your own customized automated task development environment.

Common Grunt plugins and their purposes

At this point, you should be asking yourself, what plugins can benefit me the most and why? Once you ask this question, you may find that a natural response is to ask further, what plugins are available? That is exactly the intended purpose of this section: to introduce useful grunt plugins and describe their intended purpose.

Linting JavaScript – contrib-jshint

To know more about contrib-jshint, you can refer `https://www.npmjs.com/package/grunt-contrib-jshint`:

* `grunt jshint`: This lints JavaScript files manually

The contrib-jshint plugin is to run automated JavaScript error detection and will help with identifying potential problems with your code that may surface during runtime. When the plugin is run, it will scan your JavaScript code and issue warnings on preconfigured options. There are a large number of error messages that jshint might provide, and it can be difficult at times to understand exactly what a particular message might be referring to. Some examples are as follows:

- The array literal notation [] is preferable
- {a} is already defined
- Avoid arguments {a}
- Bad assignment
- Confusing minuses

The list goes on. There are resources such as http://jslinterrors.com/ whose purpose is to help you understand what a particular warning/error message means.

Installation of contrib-jshint follows the same pattern as other plugins, using NPM to install the plugin in your project:

```
npm install grunt-contrib-jshint --save-dev
```

This will install the contrib-jshint plugin in your project's node-modules directory and register the plugin in your devDependencies section of the package.json file at the root of your project. It will be similar to the following:

```
"devDependencies": {
    "grunt": "~0.4.5",
    "grunt-contrib-jshint": "~0.4.5"
}
```

The contrib-jshint plugin is jshint, so any of the options available in jshint can be passed into contrib-jshint. Take a look at http://jshint.com/docs/options/ for a complete listing of jshint options. Some examples of options are as follows:

- `curly`: This enforces that curly braces are used in code blocks
- `undef`: This ensures that all variables have been declared
- `maxparams`: This checks to make sure that the number of arguments in a method do not exceed a specified amount

The contrib-jshint allows you to configure which files will be linted, the order in which the linting will occur, and even control the linting before and after concatenation. Additionally, contrib-jshint allows you to suppress warnings in the configuration options using the `ignore_warning` option.

Minifying Javascript – contrib-uglify

To know more about contrib-uglify, you can refer `https://www.npmjs.com/package/grunt-contrib-uglify`:

- `grunt uglify`: This minifies JavaScript files manually

Compression and minification is important to reduce file sizes and contribute to better loading times to improve performance. The contrib-uglify plugin provides the compression and minification utility by optimizing JavaScript code and removing unnecessary line breaks and whitespace. It does this by parsing JavaScript and outputting regenerated, optimized code with shortened variable names, for example.

The `contrib-uglify` plugin is installed in your project using the NPM install command, just as you will see with all other Grunt plugins:

```
npm install grunt-contrib-uglify --save-dev
```

You should see something similar to the following in `devDependencies`:

```
"devDependencies": {
    "grunt": "~0.4.5",
    "grunt-contrib-uglify": "~0.4.0"
}
```

The `contrib-uglify` plugin is configured to process specific files as defined in the gruntfile.js configuration file. Additionally, contrib-uglify will have defined output destination files that will be created for the processed minified JavaScript. There is also a beautify option that can be used to revert minified code, should you wish to debug your JavaScript more easily.

A useful option that is available in contrib-uglify is banners. Banners allow you to configure banner comments to be added to the minified output files. For example, a banner could be created with the current date and time, author, version number, and any other important information that should be included. You can reference your package.json file in order to get information, such as the package name and version, directly from the package.json configuration file. This will look like the following:

```
pkg: grunt.file.readJSON('package.json')
```

This creates a `pkg` object whose properties are the contents of package.json. Once created, each property found in package.json can be accessed via the dot notation. For example, the project version can be accessed with pkg.version. The version property exists in package.json as `version: 0.0.1`. When accessing the version property, the value of pkg.version is equal to `0.0.1`. Take a moment and look at the sample_project's package.json in order to better understand the properties that are available.

While not specific to just contrib-uglify, another notable option is the ability to configure directory-level compiling of files. You can achieve this through configuration of the files option to use wildcard path references with a file extension, such as `**/*.js`. This is useful when you want to minify all of the contents in a directory.

Compile LESS into CSS – contrib-less

To know more about contrib-less, you can refer to `https://www.npmjs.com/package/grunt-contrib-less`:

- `grunt less`: This compiles LESS to CSS manually

The contrib-less is a plugin that compiles LESS files to CSS files. LESS provides extensibility to standard CSS by allowing variables, mixins (declaring a group of style declarations at once that can be reused anywhere in the stylesheet), and even conditional logic to manage styles throughout the document.

Just as with other plugins, contrib-less is installed in your project using the `npm install` command with the following command:

```
npm install grunt-contrib-less –save-dev
```

As we are using `--save-dev`, the task will be registered in `devDependencies` of package.json. The registration will look something similar to the following:

```
"devDependencies": {
    "grunt": "~0.4.5",
    "grunt-contrib-less": "~0.4.5"
}
```

The contrib-less will be configured, using the path and file options, to define the location of source and destination output files. It can also be configured with multiple environment type options, for example, dev, test, and production, in order to apply different options that may be needed for different environments.

Some typical options used in contrib-less include the following:

- `paths`: These are the directories that should be scanned
- `compress`: This is whether to compress output to remove whitespace
- `plugins`: This is the mechanism to include additional plugins in the flow of processing
- `banner`: This is the banner to use in the compiled destination files

There are several more options not listed here; be sure to see the documentation for the full listing of contrib-less options and example usage.

Desktop notifications for automated tasks – notify

To know more about notify plugin, you can refer to `https://www.npmjs.com/package/grunt-notify`.

Notice the lack of the `contrib` prefix on this plugin. The notify is the first plugin we have discussed that is not maintained by the Grunt team, but rather by a third-party contributor of Grunt plugins.

The notify plugin integrates with your system notifications, such as Growl, OSX Notification Center, Windows 8 Notifications, Snarl, and Notify-Send, to provide you with updates on task status that you can define.

Even though notify is a third-party plugin, installation is the same as any `contrib` plugin, using the same syntax:

```
npm install grunt-notify -save-dev
```

There are also no differences in where it gets installed and registered. You will find the grunt-notify plugin installed in your node-modules directory at the root of your application along with the registration of the module in your `devDependencies` section of package.json. The entry in package.json will look something like the following:

```
"devDependencies": {
    "grunt": "~0.4.5",
    "grunt-notify": "~0.4.1"
}
```

The notify plugin is intended to be run and watch other tasks, so it is configured in gruntfile.js to run as an automated task. Once installed and loaded in gruntfile. js, there is nothing else that is required to configure; however, notify has a couple of `notify_hooks` task options that allow you to change the default messaging. These are as follows:

- **title**: This is the notification title
- **message**: This is the notification message

We will get into the actual implementation of plugins when we discuss gruntfile.js. Suffice it to say that at this point, in order to implement the `notify_hooks` options, you will configure a `notify_hooks` task in gruntfile.js. Don't be concerned with any further details at this point; we will get there soon enough.

Opening files and URLs automatically – open

To know more about the open plugin, you can refer to `https://www.npmjs.com/package/grunt-open`.

The open plugin is another plugin that is not officially supported by the Grunt team but is provided by a third-party contributor. What the open plugin does for us is it opens files and URLs as configured in a Grunt task. An example use case for open is to automatically open a browser with your running application once it has finished building.

Installation for open is typical, using the same install command syntax as we do for all other plugins:

```
npm install grunt-open –save-dev
```

The plugin registration in package.json will be found in the `devDependencies` section and looks similar to the following:

```
"devDependencies": {
    "grunt": "~0.4.5",
    "grunt-open": "~0.2.3"
}
```

The open plugin is run as part of the automated task configuration and will be used between two other tasks, server and watch. There are only two parameters and the plugin is very simply configured to specify the following:

- `path`: This is the file path or URL that will be opened
- `app`: This is the application (browser) that will be launched (if not specified, the system default browser will be used)

There are a couple of options as well:

- `openOn`: This will delay the opening of the configured path until after another Grunt process
- `delay`: This is a timed delay for the opening of the configured path

Optimizing images – contrib-imagemin

To know more about contrib-imagemin, you can refer to `https://www.npmjs.com/package/grunt-contrib-imagemin`:

- `grunt imagemin`: This minifies images manually

With this plugin, we return to an officially supported plugin that is maintained by the Grunt team. This is a useful plugin in that it compresses images without sacrificing quality, thus allowing us to optimize images and improve application image loading performance. The `contrib-imagemin` plugin will compress images in the following formats: .gif, .jpg, .png, and .svg. It is recommended that another plugin, grunt-newer, be used so that only files that have changed are processed. Compression of images can take a great deal of time, depending upon the number and size of the image files. We will cover grunt-newer next.

Installation of contrib-imagemin is accomplished with the same npm install command:

```
npm install grunt-contrib-imagemin --save-dev
```

The plugin will be registered in the devDependencies section of package.json, as we would expect when using `--save-dev`. When completed, the entry in `devDependencies` will be similar to the following:

```
"devDependencies": {
    "grunt": "~0.4.5",
    "grunt-contrib-imagemin": "~0.9.4"
}
```

Notable options of this plugin include the following:

- `optimizationLevel`: This is a number between 0-7 with 7 being the highest level of optimization for .png images

- `progressive`: This is lossless conversion to progressive .jpg to improve image loading performance

- `interlaced`: This provides interlaced .gif for progressive loading that improves rendering performance

- `svgoPlugins`: This allows the customization of .svg plugins that are used in the .svg optimization process, achieved by enabling/disabling the available .svg plugins

Running tasks only on files that changed – newer

To know more about the newer plugin, you can refer to `https://www.npmjs.com/package/grunt-newer`.

As mentioned in the last plugin, the `newer` plugin controls running tasks only on files whose source files have changed since the last successful completion of the task or whose source file is newer than the destination file. Using the example of contrib-imagemin, processing the compression of images can be a lengthy process, especially if compression levels are high. The newer plugin helps optimize the running of tasks by running them only on files that have changed or are newer than the destination files that they would replace.

Installation of newer is accomplished with the following `npm install` command:

```
npm install grunt-newer --save-dev
```

Following the installation of the plugin, your `devDependencies` should resemble the following example:

```
"devDependencies": {
    "grunt": "~0.4.5",
    "grunt-newer": "~1.1.1"
}
```

The newer plugin can be used without configuration other than simply adding the newer task argument prior to other task arguments. When placed before the other tasks, these tasks will run only if newer detects that the source files defined by the upcoming task have changed since the last successful task run or the source files are newer than the destination files. Additionally, as newer manages the running of tasks based on if a source file is newer than the last successful task completion, newer will work for tasks that do not have any destination file output. The contrib-jshint is a good example of a task that does not produce any destination files. It is not necessary to run jshint on a file again if that file has not changed since the last successful completion of the task. The newer plugin has minimal options:

- `cache`: This defines a custom cache directory location
- `override`: This allows tasks to run on a file even though it has not been modified

Performing SSH and SFTP tasks – ssh

To know more about SSH, you can refer to `https://www.npmjs.com/package/grunt-ssh`:

The SSH is a third-party plugin that provides SSH and SFTP tasks from Grunt. A typical use case would be to securely transfer deployment files to a remote dev, test, or production server. SSH and SFTP operations are performed by separate tasks that are included with the ssh plugin. These are the SFTP and sshexec tasks.

Installation of the SSH plugin is accomplished via the `npm install` command using the following:

```
npm install grunt-ssh --save-dev
```

When complete, you should expect to see an entry similar to the following:

```
"devDependencies": {
    "grunt": "~0.4.5",
    "grunt-ssh": "~0.12.6"
}
```

One or both sshexec and/or SFTP operations can be configured. For an SFTP copy of files to a remote server, you will have the following configuration parameters:

- `files`: These are the files that will be copied as key-value pairs where key is the path and value is the file or array of files to be copied

There are some options that will need to be configured as well:

- `username`: This is the remote server username credential
- `password`: This is the remote server password credential
- `host`: This is the remote host that files will transfer to
- `port`: This is the ssh port to use

A credentials.json file can be created so that sensitive credentials are not shared across version control. The gruntfile can then read the credentials.json file as follows:

```
{
    "host" : "remoteHost",
    "username" : "myUserName",
    "password" : "myPassword"
}
```

- The sshexec configuration is similar and may use the same strategy to secure sensitive credential information that is used to authenticate to remote servers. With the sshexec task, you can run `ssh` commands from the automated task. There is one parameter for sshexec:

- `command`: This is one or multiple (array) commands to issue to the remote server

Like sftp, options for sshexec include the following:

- `username`: This is the remote server username credential
- `password`: This is the remote server password credential
- `host`: This is the remote host that files will transfer to
- `port`: This is the ssh port to use

There are several additional options available; here are a few for example:

- `options`: This is one of three connection options — privateKey, password, and agent
- `passphrase`: This is the passphrase for the private key
- `agent`: This is the path to the ssh-agents Unix socket
- `readyTimeout`: This is the number of milliseconds to wait before timeout occurs waiting on completion of the SSH handshake

The minification of CSS – contrib-cssmin

To know more about contrib-cssmin plugin, you can refer to `https://www.npmjs.com/package/grunt-contrib-cssmin`.

- `grunt cssmin`: This minifies CSS files manually

The contrib-cssmin is a plugin to minify CSS files in order to reduce file size and increase performance. It parses CSS files to remove whitespace, comments, empty style declarations, and blocks. The parsed files are then output to minified destination files.

The contrib-cssmin plugin is installed with the `npm install` command as follows:

```
npm install grunt-contrib-cssmin --save-dev
```

An entry will be added to the `devDependencies` section of your package.json file and will be similar to this:

```
"devDependencies": {
    "grunt": "~0.4.5",
    "grunt-contrib-cssmin": "~0.13.0"
}
```

This plugin uses a Node.js library named clean-css. Options for clean-css are defined in the contrib-cssmin configuration in your gruntfile.js that we will discuss later. You will find all of the available options for clean-css at `https://github.com/jakubpawlowicz/clean-css#how-to-use-clean-css-api`. Using the clean-css configuration options, you can customize the minification of your CSS files.

Basic usage of contrib-cssmin includes the concatenation of CSS files into a single file and minification of CSS file contents. Some available options are as follows:

- `banner`: This defines a banner to be placed in the compressed file
- `keepSpeacialComments`: This keeps or removes special comments (uses the clean-css option)
- `report`: This reports minification or gzip results

Some of the available configuration parameters are as follows:

- `combine`: This combines two files into one destination file
- `minify`: This minifies contents into a specified destination directory

Concatenate files – contrib-concat

To know more about contrib-concat plugin, you can refer to `https://www.npmjs.com/package/grunt-contrib-concat`:

- `grunt concat`: This concatenates files manually

The purpose of contrib-concat is to concatenate multiple files into a single file. For instance, part of your workflow may require that all JavaScript source files be combined into a single production deployment file. The contrib-concat plugin will allow you to define all of the files to be concatenated, specify any separator that may be needed (it may be necessary to separate JavaScript files with a semicolon, for example), and configure the destination file that will be created with the concatenated files from source.

As with all of the plugins that we have seen, contrib-concat is installed using the npm install command:

```
npm install grunt-contrib-concat --save-dev
```

The plugin will be registered in your devDependencies section of package.json and will resemble the following:

```
"devDependencies": {
    "grunt": "~0.4.5",
    "grunt-contrib-concat": "~0.5.1"
}
```

There are quite a few options:

- separator: This is the string to be used to separate files, for example, a semicolon

- banner: This is the banner to add to the concatenated destination file

- footer: This is the string to be added to the end of the concatenated destination file

- stripBanners: This removes JavaScript banner comments from the source files

- process: This processes files prior to concatenation

- sourceMap: This creates a source file map if set to true

- sourceMapName: This adds a custom name for the generated source map

- sourceMapStyle: This configures the type of source map that will be created, for example, embedded (directly in the source map), link (referenced as links), or inline (entire map stored in the output file)

Cleaning up files and folders – contrib-clean

To know more about contrib-clean plugin, you can refer to https://www.npmjs.com/package/grunt-contrib-clean:

- grunt clean: This cleans files and directories manually

The contrib-clean plugin takes care of housecleaning by keeping files and folders cleaned up. You can specify the directories and even individual files that you would like to be deleted and can also define files and directories that should not be deleted. Obviously, this plugin should be used with caution. There is an option that will log what would have happened rather than actually perform the file and/or directory deletions.

Installation of contrib-clean is accomplished with the NPM install command:

```
npm install grunt-contrib-clean --save-dev
```

The plugin will be registered in the devDependencies section of your package.json file and will resemble the following:

```
"devDependencies": {
    "grunt": "~0.4.5",
    "grunt-contrib-clean": "~0.6.0"
}
```

There are only a couple of options for the configuration of contrib-clean:

- force: This is an override of blocking deletions from outside the current working directory
- no-write: This creates log messages of what would have happened rather than actually deleting files and/or folders

The contrib-clean plugin provides three formats to run the task: short, medium, and long. Additionally, it is possible to configure skipping files with the use of the ! operator. An example of usage for the skipping might be when you have a directory of generated source files that were minified and concatenated into a destination file. A common pattern is to build all of the distribution files into a dist directory. Upon each build for distribution, it is necessary to clean the dist directory. This can be accomplished by removing the dist directory entirely or recursively removing all files and directories from within the dist directory. You could specify all of the generated source files to be deleted but not (!) the destination file. You might accomplish this with a special prefix, such as *.min.js, which would differentiate the concatenated file from the *.js source files.

Minifying HTML files – contrib-htmlmin

To know more about contrib-htmlmin plugin, you can refer to https://www.npmjs. com/package/grunt-contrib-htmlmin:

- grunt htmlmin: This minifies HTML files manually

The contrib-htmlmin plugin minifies HTML files, much the same as we would expect from CSS or JS file minification that we have previously covered. The contrib-htmlmin plugin can be configured to remove comments and collapse whitespace, which are the two options that it uses in order to compress HTML files. It uses the html-minifier library; documentation on this library can be found at https://github.com/kangax/html-minifier#options-quick-reference.

The contrib-htmlmin plugin is installed using the `npm install` command:

```
npm install grunt-contrib-htmlmin --save-dev
```

The plugin will be registered in your `devDependencies` section of package.json and will be similar to the following:

```
"devDependencies": {
    "grunt": "~0.4.5",
    "grunt-contrib-htmlmin": "~0.4.0"
}
```

The available options are from the html-minifier library as referenced in the preceding link. Some examples of options that can be used to configure contrib-htmlmin are:

- `removeComments`: This removes comments from the source HTML files
- `collapseWhitespace`: This removes the whitespace characters from the document
- `removeAttributeQuotes`: This removes quotes surrounding HTML attributes when possible
- `removeEmptyElements`: This removes all elements without contents
- `minifyJS`: This minifies JavaScript within script elements
- `minifyCSS`: This minifies CSS within style tags and elements
- `minifyURLs`: This minifies URL attributes

Watch for changing files - contrib-watch

To know more about contrib-watch plugin, you can refer to `https://www.npmjs.com/package/grunt-contrib-watch`:

- `grunt watch`: This starts watching files manually. It will continue to watch until you end your session.

This is, in my opinion, probably the most useful plugin available. The contrib-watch plugin responds to changes in files defined by you and runs additional tasks upon being triggered by the changed file events. For example, let's say that you make changes to a JavaScript file. When you save and these changes are persisted, contrib-watch will detect that the file being watched has changed. An example workflow might be to make and save changes to a JavaScript file and then run Lint on the file. You might paste code in a Lint tool, such as http://www.jslint.com/, or you might run an editor plugin tool on the file to ensure that your code is valid and has no defined errors. Using Grunt and contrib-watch, you can configure contrib-watch to automatically run a Grunt linting plugin so that every time you make changes to your JavaScript files, they are automatically linted.

Installation of contrib-watch is straightforward, as described in *Obtaining Grunt plugin* section in this chapter and accomplished using the npm-install command:

```
npm install grunt-contrib-watch –save-dev
```

Take a look at the Angular Seed project for an example, something similar will be found in package.json when you actually run that command:

```
"devDependencies": {
    "grunt": "~0.4.5",
    "grunt-contrib-watch": "~0.4.0"
}
```

> Notice the tilde character (~) in the "grunt-contrib-watch": "0.5.3" line. The tilde actually specifies that the most recent minor version should be used when updating. So, for instance, if you updated your npm package for the project, it would use 0.5.4 if it was available; however, it would not use 0.6.x as that is a higher minor version. There is also a caret character (^) that you may see. It will allow updates matching the most recent major version. In the case of the 0.5.3 example, 0.6.3 would be allowed while 1.x versions would not. For more information and documentation on the library that parses the versioning, refer to node-semver, located at https://github.com/npm/node-semver.

At this point, contrib-watch is ready to be configured in your project within what is called a Gruntfile. We will look more into the gruntfile in later chapters. It should be noted that this, and many other tasks, can be run manually.

The contrib-watch plugin has some useful options. While we won't cover all of the available options, the following are some notables that you should be aware of. Be sure to review the documentation for the full listing of options:

- `options.event`
- `options.reload`
- `options.livereload`

The `Options.event` method will allow you to configure contrib-watch to only trigger when certain types of events occur. The available types are `all`, `changed`, `added`, and `deleted`. You can configure more than one type if you wish. The `all` will trigger any file change, `added` will respond to new files added, and `deleted` will be triggered on removal of a file.

The `Options.reload` method will trigger the reload of the watch task when any of the watched files change. A good example of this is when the Gruntfile in which watch is configured changes. This will reload the Gruntfile. The contrib-watch will continue watching for additional changes and respond to them when they occur.

The `Options.livereload` method is different than reload, so don't confuse the two. Livereload starts a server that enables live reloading. What this means is that when files are changed, your server will automatically update with the changed files. Take, for instance, a web application running in a browser. Rather than saving your files and then having to refresh your browser to get the changed files, livereload automatically reloads your app in the browser for you.

Summary

You have discovered many plugins, their purposes, and some of their details. While it seems like we have covered quite a bit, what we have discovered here is a small sample of the available plugins that exist to be used in a myriad of project types for various workflow purposes. Plugins are core to Grunt and are the building blocks to automated workflows. Each plugin has its own unique configuration parameters and options, allowing the customization of tasks to suit the needs of individual project workflows and requirements. You have been introduced to some common tasks in an effort to become aware of what types of tasks are available, where to find them, and details of what these tasks will do for you.

Grunt plugins can most easily be searched for and obtained by visiting the Grunt plugins page, found at `http://gruntjs.com/plugins`. A link to each plugin NPM page has been provided under each plugin header. Plugins can be differentiated by whether they are officially supported or maintained by third-party contributors. Officially supported plugins are distinguishable by the `contrib-` prefix and denoted with a star icon on the Grunt plugins page. Plugins that are not officially maintained by the Grunt team are provided by organizations and individuals. These are developed and shared in order to benefit the community. They may have developed them in order to solve their own workflow problems or perhaps just as an idea that might be a resource for the community; in either case, they are there for you to use in your projects as you see fit.

In the next chapter, we will begin looking at the configuration of Grunt tasks, which will involve gruntfile.js and package.json that has been mentioned so often in this chapter. Once we have the opportunity to learn about configuration, return to this chapter for reference for some of the parameters, options of specific plugins, and links to additional resources.

Configuration of Grunt Tasks

4

In the previous chapter, an assortment of Grunt tasks were introduced, and information was provided to become familiar with how to obtain plugins as well as the syntax used to add plugins to your project. In this chapter, we will look at the actual installation and configuration of grunt tasks using the Angular Seed project. There will be two main files that we will be focusing closely on: package.json and gruntfile.js. These two files are where the grunt configuration takes place, some of it automatically, such as when we install a plugin and the package.json file is updated, as shown in the examples in *Chapter 3, All about Grunt Plugins*. Other configuration is completed manually so that plugin behavior can be defined- and customized as per the project's requirements.

- Reviewing the installation of Grunt tasks
- Discussing package.json and gruntfile.js
- Introducing the Grunt API

Reviewing the installation of Grunt tasks

In each task that was outlined in *Chapter 3, All about Grunt Plugins* there was a distinctly common thread that existed between all of the plugins: the installation process. Installation of plugins is accomplished through Terminal or command line, and the syntax is very simple. As previously described, here is the common format of the task installation syntax for grunt plugins:

```
npm install [package name] --save-dev
```

The `npm install` command invokes the installation of a package, `[package name]`. Additionally, this command has an optional flag, `-save-dev`, which instructs the installer to save the package as a development dependency. Plugins saved as devDependencies are saved locally to the project and registered in the package.json file in the devDependencies configuration section. The plugin itself, when installed as a devDependencies configuration, will be located in your project's node-modules directory. In this section, we will be installing plugins in the Angular Seed project note that the installation order of plugins is not important).

Installing contrib-jshint with NPM

As mentioned previously, one of the repetitive tasks that we will want to configure to run in our automated build will be linting our JavaScript. We will need the contrib-jshint plugin to perform this work for us. As has been shown, the installation process from plugin to plugin is virtually the same. We will perform the same process and have a look at the results of the installation process. Ensure that you are in the root of the sample_project directory:

```
cd [Your Project Directory]
```

As before, once confirmed that we are in the root of our sample_project directory, run the NPM install command for contrib-jshint:

```
npm install grunt-contrib-jshint –save-dev
```

Your output should be similar to the following contrib-jshint installation log. If you have a look at the output, you will see that some additional packages have been installed along with the plugin and all of the packages that we are installing. These additional packages are plugin dependencies that are required by the plugin. So, in the case of contrib-jshint, note that strip-json-comments, exit, shelljs, console-browserfy, minimatch, cli, lodash, and htmlparser have all been installed as dependencies of jshint. You can find these additional packages in the npm directory, `https://www.npmjs.com/`, in order to learn more about each one. For instance, strip-json-comments allow you to use comments in your json files and then strip them out at build time. You can find information about strip-json-comments at `https://www.npmjs.com/package/strip-json-comments`:

```
○ ○ ○                    🗀 sample_project — bash — 84×29
drcsoft-mbp:sample_project dougrdotnet$ npm install grunt-contrib-jshint --save-dev
grunt-contrib-jshint@0.11.3 node_modules/grunt-contrib-jshint
├── hooker@0.2.3
└── jshint@2.8.0 (strip-json-comments@1.0.4, exit@0.1.2, shelljs@0.3.0, console-brow
serify@1.1.0, minimatch@2.0.10, cli@0.6.6, lodash@3.7.0, htmlparser2@3.8.3)
drcsoft-mbp:sample_project dougrdotnet$ ▌
```

Installation will automatically update our package.json file, registering contrib-jshint in devDependencies:

```
"devDependencies": {
    "bower": "^1.3.1",
    "grunt": "^0.4.5",
    "grunt-contrib-jshint": "^0.11.3",
    "grunt-contrib-watch": "^0.6.1",
    "http-server": "^0.6.1",
    "jasmine-core": "^2.3.4",
    "karma": "~0.12",
    "karma-chrome-launcher": "^0.1.12",
    "karma-firefox-launcher": "^0.1.6",
    "karma-jasmine": "^0.3.5",
    "karma-junit-reporter": "^0.2.2",
    "protractor": "^2.1.0",
    "shelljs": "^0.2.6"
}
```

As expected, contrib-jshint is installed in the node-modules directory located at the root of the sample_project directory:

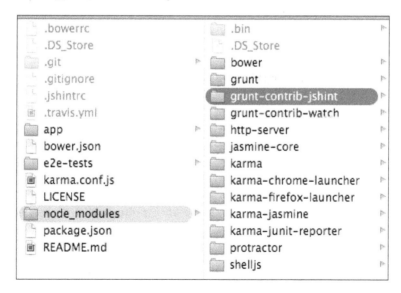

This is all that needs to be done in order to install the contrib-jshint plugin in sample_project. The plugin is now ready to be configured in gruntfile.js; however, we will continue to install more plugins at this point. We will focus on configuration later on, without the interruption of installing plugins. It should be noted that it is perfectly fine to install plugins and configure, then later install more plugins and modify the gruntfile.js configuration. These steps can be repeated over and over to continually meet the requirements of your project. One of the beauties of Grunt is that it allows you to modify and scale your build requirements with your project as your project's needs evolve.

Installing contrib-uglify with NPM

As we progress through our build process, we will want to compress or minify our JavaScript so that we can decrease loading time and improve performance. The contrib-uglify plugin handles this compression with the optimization of JavaScript code, removal of unneeded whitespace, shortening of variable names, and other parsing operations, in order to reduce file size. The installation process is, again, the same as what we have been performing thus far. First, if you aren't already in your project directory, change directories to the root of your sample_project:

```
cd [Your Project Directory]
```

Once in the root of your sample_project, run the npm install command to install contrib-uglify in your project:

```
npm install grunt-contrib-uglify –save-dev
```

After running the install command, your console output should be similar to the following:

```
○ ○ ○                    sample_project — bash — 84×29
drcsoft-mbp:sample_project dougrdotnet$ npm install grunt-contrib-uglify –save-dev
grunt-contrib-uglify@0.9.2 node_modules/grunt-contrib-uglify
├── uri-path@0.0.2
├── chalk@1.1.1 (supports-color@2.0.0, escape-string-regexp@1.0.3, ansi-styles@2.1.0
, strip-ansi@3.0.0, has-ansi@2.0.0)
├── uglify-js@2.4.24 (uglify-to-browserify@1.0.2, async@0.2.10, yargs@3.5.4, source-
map@0.1.34)
├── lodash@3.10.1
└── maxmin@1.1.0 (figures@1.4.0, gzip-size@1.0.0, pretty-bytes@1.0.4)
drcsoft-mbp:sample_project dougrdotnet$ 
```

As we would expect, package.json will have been updated to add the registration of contrib-uglify to the `devDependencies` section:

```
"devDependencies": {
    "bower": "^1.3.1",
    "grunt": "^0.4.5",
    "grunt-contrib-jshint": "^0.11.3",
    "grunt-contrib-uglify": "^0.9.2",
    "grunt-contrib-watch": "^0.6.1",
    "http-server": "^0.6.1",
    "jasmine-core": "^2.3.4",
    "karma": "~0.12",
    "karma-chrome-launcher": "^0.1.12",
    "karma-firefox-launcher": "^0.1.6",
    "karma-jasmine": "^0.3.5",
    "karma-junit-reporter": "^0.2.2",
    "protractor": "^2.1.0",
    "shelljs": "^0.2.6"
}
```

A quick inspection of our sample_project's node-modules directory should confirm that the contrib-uglify package has been successfully installed:

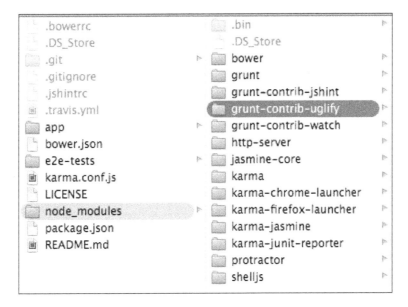

Installing contrib-less with NPM

The sample_project will illustrate the use of LESS, which provides extensibility to CSS through the use of variables, mixins, and conditional logic. The contrib-less task handles the compilation of LESS files into CSS. An additional bonus is that we can use contrib-less to handle our CSS minification to help reduce file size. As we have done in each package installation, ensure that you are in the root of your sample_project directory, if not, change directories to the project root:

```
cd [Your Project Directory]
```

Once confirmed that you are in the root of your project, run the npm install command in order to install contrib-less in sample_project:

```
npm install grunt-contrib-less –save-dev
```

When the install command is completed, you should see a console output similar to the following:

```
drcsoft-mbp:sample_project dougrdotnet$ npm install grunt-contrib-less –save-dev
grunt-contrib-less@1.0.1 node_modules/grunt-contrib-less
├── async@0.9.2
├── lodash@2.4.2
├── chalk@0.5.1 (ansi-styles@1.1.0, escape-string-regexp@1.0.3, supports-color@0.2.0
, strip-ansi@0.3.0, has-ansi@0.1.0)
└── less@2.4.0 (graceful-fs@3.0.8, mime@1.3.4, image-size@0.3.5, mkdirp@0.5.1, sourc
e-map@0.2.0, errno@0.1.4, promise@6.1.0, request@2.64.0)
drcsoft-mbp:sample_project dougrdotnet$
```

Note that package.json has been updated with the contrib-less registration:

```
"devDependencies": {
    "bower": "^1.3.1",
    "grunt": "^0.4.5",
    "grunt-contrib-jshint": "^0.11.3",
    "grunt-contrib-less": "^1.0.1",
    "grunt-contrib-uglify": "^0.9.2",
    "grunt-contrib-watch": "^0.6.1",
    "http-server": "^0.6.1",
    "jasmine-core": "^2.3.4",
    "karma": "~0.12",
    "karma-chrome-launcher": "^0.1.12",
    "karma-firefox-launcher": "^0.1.6",
    "karma-jasmine": "^0.3.5",
```

```
    "karma-junit-reporter": "^0.2.2",
    "protractor": "^2.1.0",
    "shelljs": "^0.2.6"
}
```

The contrib-less package should now be installed in the sample_project's node-modules directory:

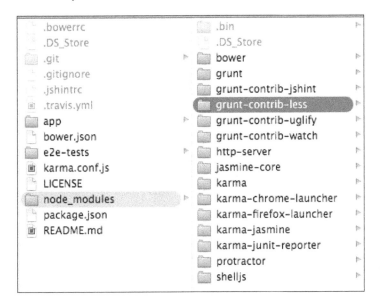

Installing contrib-watch with NPM

The first plugin that we will install is the contrib-watch task. This detects file changes and responds to these events by running additional configured tasks. The configuration takes place in gruntfile.js. To put this in a clearer perspective, our project will have JavaScript files that be modified frequently. Every time we save modifications, we want to run jshint on the files to lint them for errors. Rather than having to do this manually each time, we will configure contrib-watch to automate the linting process for us. More on this configuration later; for now, let's just get contrib-watch installed.

Open a command prompt and change directories to your Angular Seed sample project root directory that we created in *Chapter 2, Foundation for Creating an app using Angular.JS*:

```
cd [Your Project Directory]
```

Once we are in our project directory, we can simply install contrib-watch with the following npm command:

```
npm install grunt-contrib-watch –save-dev
```

Your output should look similar to the following:

```
○ ○ ○                        sample_project — bash — 80×29
grunt@0.4.5 node_modules/grunt
├── dateformat@1.0.2-1.2.3
├── which@1.0.9
├── getobject@0.1.0
├── eventemitter2@0.4.14
├── rimraf@2.2.8
├── colors@0.6.2
├── async@0.1.22
├── grunt-legacy-util@0.2.0
├── hooker@0.2.3
├── nopt@1.0.10 (abbrev@1.0.7)
├── exit@0.1.2
├── minimatch@0.2.14 (sigmund@1.0.1, lru-cache@2.7.0)
├── glob@3.1.21 (inherits@1.0.2, graceful-fs@1.2.3)
├── lodash@0.9.2
├── coffee-script@1.3.3
├── underscore.string@2.2.1
├── iconv-lite@0.2.11
├── findup-sync@0.1.3 (glob@3.2.11, lodash@2.4.2)
├── grunt-legacy-log@0.1.2 (grunt-legacy-log-utils@0.1.1, underscore.string@2.3.
3, lodash@2.4.2)
└── js-yaml@2.0.5 (esprima@1.0.4, argparse@0.1.16)

grunt-contrib-watch@0.6.1 node_modules/grunt-contrib-watch
├── async@0.2.10
├── lodash@2.4.2
├── tiny-lr-fork@0.0.5 (debug@0.7.4, faye-websocket@0.4.4, qs@0.5.6, noptify@0.0
.3)
└── gaze@0.5.1 (globule@0.1.0)
```

The devDependencies section will now look similar to this excerpt from package.json:

```
"devDependencies": {
    "bower": "^1.3.1",
    "grunt": "^0.4.5",
    "grunt-contrib-watch": "^0.6.1",
    "http-server": "^0.6.1",
    "jasmine-core": "^2.3.4",
    "karma": "~0.12",
    "karma-chrome-launcher": "^0.1.12",
    "karma-firefox-launcher": "^0.1.6",
```

```
    "karma-jasmine": "^0.3.5",
    "karma-junit-reporter": "^0.2.2",
    "protractor": "^2.1.0",
    "shelljs": "^0.2.6"
}
```

The contrib-watch plugin is now installed in the node-modules directory located at the root of the sample_project directory:

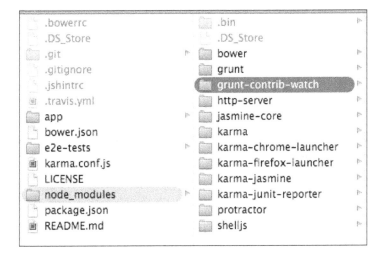

The contrib-watch plugin is now installed in sample_project and ready to be configured in gruntfile.js. Before moving on to configuration, let's continue to install additional plugins that we will need to get going.

Discussing package.json and gruntfile.js

Grunt projects have two important files that are required in order to define and configure Grunt: package.json and gruntfile.js. The package.json is a JSON file that is normally located at the root of a project using NPM to manage dependencies, and gruntfile.js is a JavaScript file that also exists in the project root directory. The combination of these two files provides the information about the project and configuration of the packages used in the project that are needed in order to create an automated build system. We will look at each in more detail before beginning to configure sample_project.

The package.json file

As mentioned, package.json is a JSON file that defines data about our project, also known as project metadata. In this file, as we have seen throughout our plugin installation process, we have registered our project's plugins in the devDependencies section.

The metadata that package.json defines, in addition to the project dependencies, is a set of properties that describes your project. Name and version are both required fields:

- **Name**: This is the name of the application. It must be shorter than 214 characters, must not start with a dot or underscore, and must not contain any non-URL-safe characters.

- **Version**: This is the version of your application. It must be able to be parsed by node-semver (`https://github.com/npm/node-semver`). The combination of the name and version is required because, together, they will create a unique application identifier.

In sample_project, there are some additional fields added during our Angular Seed project creation, which include private, description, repository, and licence:

- Private: This instructs npm to never publish your project and prevents the possibility of accidentally publishing a private repository

- Description: This is a brief excerpt that describes the project

- Repository: This is the location of the project code

- Licence: This defines how the application can be used by others

We have been watching the devDependencies section of the package.json develop as we have worked through the package installation process. The devDependencies is really just a simple JSON object whose properties define the package dependencies of our project. Notice each entry in devDependencies as it exists at this time:

```
"devDependencies": {
    "bower": "^1.3.1",
    "grunt": "^0.4.5",
    "grunt-contrib-jshint": "^0.11.3",
    "grunt-contrib-less": "^1.0.1",
    "grunt-contrib-uglify": "^0.9.2",
    "grunt-contrib-watch": "^0.6.1",
    "http-server": "^0.6.1",
    "jasmine-core": "^2.3.4",
    "karma": "~0.12",
```

```
        "karma-chrome-launcher": "^0.1.12",
        "karma-firefox-launcher": "^0.1.6",
        "karma-jasmine": "^0.3.5",
        "karma-junit-reporter": "^0.2.2",
        "protractor": "^2.1.0",
        "shelljs": "^0.2.6"
    }
```

Each line defined in the `devDependencies` object is a map and key-value pair that matches up an application name with a version. Both the name and version are strings and the version may include a descriptor. If the version has no descriptor, then the version string must be matched exactly. If the > version descriptor is used, then the version must match any version greater than the value. Other descriptors include the following:

- `>=`: The version must be greater than or equal to the value
- `<`: The version must be less than the value
- `<=`: The version must be less than or equal to the value
- `~`: The version must be the approximate equivalent to the value
- `^`: The version must be compatible with the value
- `1.2.x`: The version may match any minor version, for example, 1.2.8
- `*`: The version may match any versions

Note that the package.json file also contains a scripts dictionary object. This object defines scripts that should be run as part of the dependency and when the script should be run. Let's look at our scripts object as an example:

```
"scripts": {
    "postinstall": "bower install",
    "prestart": "npm install",
    "start": "http-server -a localhost -p 8000 -c-1",
    "pretest": "npm install",
    "test": "karma start karma.conf.js",
    "test-single-run": "karma start karma.conf.js  --single-run",
    "preupdate-webdriver": "npm install",
    "update-webdriver": "webdriver-manager update",
    "preprotractor": "npm run update-webdriver",
    "protractor": "protractor e2e-tests/protractor.conf.js"...
truncated for brevaty
}
```

Notice that each object maps a command to a script. For example, the postinstall command is run after the package is installed, prestart is run by the npm start command, start is also run by the npm start command, and pretest, test, and test-single-run are all run by the npm test command. More information on the scripts dictionary can be found in the npm documentation at `https://docs.npmjs.com/misc/scripts`.

The gruntfile.js file

Up to this point, we have been putting off gruntfile.js as something that we will get into later. Finally, it is time to discuss gruntfile in detail. As mentioned previously, gruntfile, for the purposes of sample_project, is a valid JavaScript file. Note that it may also be written in CoffeeScript. Gruntfile should be located at the root of the project and part of your project source code.

A gruntfile will include a wrapper function that will contain all of the grunt-related code within. The wrapper function syntax looks as follows:

```
module.exports = function(grunt) {
  // grunt related code
};
```

The `module.exports` encapsulates the code within to create a single module of code. The exports object becomes the result returned when a require call is made, and `module.exports` is set equal to a function that takes a grunt object as its argument. The wrapper function will contain the following parts:

- Project and task configuration
- Loading Grunt plugins and tasks
- Custom tasks

In the wrapper method, there will be a call to the `grunt.initConfig` method. Most of the grunt plugins will use `initConfig` for configuration. In `sample_project`, one of the first items to be configured is getting the project's metadata from package. json so that we can use it in our automated build. We will get the name, version, and current date so that we can create a header banner that can be used in our build files. Here is a code example that we can walk through and discuss:

```
module.exports = function(grunt) {
  grunt.initConfig({
        pkg: grunt.file.readJSON('package.json'),
      banner: '/*! <%= pkg.name %>' + ' <%=
    grunt.template.today("yyyy-mm-dd") %> */\n',
        uglify: {
```

```
        options: {
                banner: '<%= banner %>'
        },
            ...{
            }
        }
    });
};
```

The `module.exports` object contains all of our grunt-related code. The first section of our configuration is the `grunt.initConfig` method. In `initConfig`, we created an object property named `pkg` and assigned it to the value of the metadata contained in package.json. We then created a banner property that creates a comment string. This will be used as a banner comment in the minified JavaScript created by contrib-uglify. The banner property string uses template string variables identified by `<% %>`, which will be replaced with content from package.json. The `<%= pkg. name %>` template string variable gets the value of the name property from package. json and replaces the variable with this content. When the template string variable is replaced, it will read angular-seed, which is the name of the sample_project project. Now, we get to take a sneak peak of the plugin configuration in order to show how we can use the banner in the configuration of contrib-uglify. In the following abbreviated contrib-uglify configuration, we simply need to add the banner to the configuration options:

```
uglify: {
        options: {
                banner: '<%= banner %>'
        },
            ...{
            }
        }
```

The `uglify` method takes an optional banner configuration so that a comment header may be included in the minified output files with which it creates. Lets have a the banner example:

banner: '/*! <%= pkg.name %>' + ' <%= grunt.template.today("yyyy-mm-dd") %> */\n,

The following comment will be created and added to the head of the generated minified JavaScript. The result is a template string variable replacement and concatenation of the name and date, obtained from the `grunt .today` method:

/*! angular-seed 2015-09-28 */

Moving beyond task configuration and into loading Grunt plugins, we need to understand the prerequisites of loading a plugin. All of the work that we have done thus far in installing plugins has created our plugin mappings in devDependencies. The plugin will be installed in the node-modules directory using npm install. Once the plugin exists in node-modules and is mapped in devDependencies, then it may be loaded in gruntfile.js. Loading, or enabling, a plugin is very simple and only takes a single line of code. The following is the code needed in order to load contrib-uglify:

```
grunt.loadNpmTasks('grunt-contrib-uglify');
```

Loading plugins takes place below the grunt.initConfig method, following its closing brace. For instance, loading contrib-uglify would look something like this:

```
module.exports = function(grunt) {
  grunt.initConfig({
        pkg: grunt.file.readJSON('package.json'),
      ...
    });
    grunt.loadNpmTasks('grunt-contrib-uglify');
};
```

In Grunt, you can define a task to run as the default task. In fact, you can define multiple tasks to run as the default task. This is known as creating a custom task. When you define a custom default task, it will always run if nothing else is defined. Recall that each task had its own command that could be used to run the task from the command line manually. The contrib-uglify command can be run manually by issuing the grunt uglify command. Notice that we use the grunt command and then specify the task to be run. If we were to run the grunt command by itself, with a default task defined, it would run automatically. We can create a default command that controls the order with which our plugins run and only have to issue the grunt command to invoke our build process, if we so desire.

Let's take a look at how we create a custom task. First, lets look at the scenario that we just outlined and create a custom task that will automatically run contrib-uglify as the default task. The syntax to create a custom task is also simple. Here is our default task example:

```
grunt.registerTask('default', ['uglify']);
```

Here, we simply register the task, define it as default, and provide an array of tasks to be run. In this case, our array only has a single item. Did you catch that? As the `registerTask` method takes an array of tasks as an argument, we can define multiple tasks to run as our default task. What if we wanted to lint our JavaScript, then minify the linted scripts, and then compile our LESS into CSS, all in one build command? This would be very simple using the `registerTask` method:

```
grunt.registerTask('default', ['jshint','uglify','less']);
```

Custom tasks aren't just limited to grunt plugins. Custom JavaScript can be used in a custom task. Javascript methods can be included in the `registerTask` method as follows:

```
grunt.registerTask('default', 'myTaskName', function() {
    //some javascript here
});
```

It is also possible to load external JavaScript files using the `grunt.loadTasks` method. The syntax to use this method is as follows:

```
grunt.task.loadTasks(pathToFile)
```

You can also use the following method:

```
grunt.loadTasks(pathToFile)
```

Grunt provides a sample gruntfile that can be used to get started quickly. While the sample may not be exactly what is needed, it is a good way to get started quickly with a configuration file that can be easily modified to meet project needs. To get started, we can get the sample gruntfile js from the source:

```
module.exports = function(grunt) {

  grunt.initConfig({
    pkg: grunt.file.readJSON('package.json'),
    concat: {
      options: {
        separator: ';'
      },
      dist: {
        src: ['src/**/*.js'],
        dest: 'dist/<%= pkg.name %>.js'
      }
    },
    uglify: {
      options: {
```

```
          banner: '/*! <%= pkg.name %> <%= grunt.template.today("dd-mm-
yyyy") %> */\n'
        },
        dist: {
          files: {
            'dist/<%= pkg.name %>.min.js': ['<%= concat.dist.dest %>']
          }
        }
      },
      qunit: {
        files: ['test/**/*.html']
      },
      jshint: {
        files: ['Gruntfile.js', 'src/**/*.js', 'test/**/*.js'],
        options: {
          // options here to override JSHint defaults
          globals: {
            jQuery: true,
            console: true,
            module: true,
            document: true
          }
        }
      },
      watch: {
        files: ['<%= jshint.files %>'],
        tasks: ['jshint', 'qunit']
      }
    });

  grunt.loadNpmTasks('grunt-contrib-uglify');
  grunt.loadNpmTasks('grunt-contrib-jshint');
  grunt.loadNpmTasks('grunt-contrib-qunit');
  grunt.loadNpmTasks('grunt-contrib-watch');
  grunt.loadNpmTasks('grunt-contrib-concat');

  grunt.registerTask('test', ['jshint', 'qunit']);

  grunt.registerTask('default', ['jshint', 'qunit', 'concat',
'uglify']);

};
```

Hopefully, the amount of content in the file isn't of concern; each section has already been discussed. Looking at the sample gruntfile.js, let's break it down section by section. Notice that everything in gruntfile.js is enclosed in the wrapper. At the top of the document, we have our `grunt.initConfig` method where all of our plugin configuration takes place.

The contents of package.json are imported to the `pkg` property so that we can get at the values defined in package.json, such as name, description, and version.

This configuration uses `grunt-contrib-concat`. The purpose of `contrib-concat` is to concatenate multiple files into a single file. It is important to be sure to use the correct separator when concatenating JavaScript files, so the options configuration defines a semicolon as the separator option. The `dist` options defines the source files to be concatenated and the destination files where the concatenated output will be written. Then, we have a closing brace and comma, which leads us to our next plugin configuration.

Next, contrib-uglify is configured to use the optional banner so that it will automatically include header comments in the minified output file. The `dist` option defines the filenames for source and destination and also uses template string variables for dynamic file naming within the files configuration:

```
files: {
    'dist/<%= pkg.name %>.min.js': ['<%= concat.dist.dest %>']
}
```

The files parameter defines the path to source, such as `dist/angular-seed.min.js`, and concatenates it with the file that was produced from the concat plugin (concat.dist.dest).

The sample gruntfile configures the contrib-qunit task that simply runs the unit test files. It takes a files parameter to define the path to the test runner; the asterisks are path wildcards:

```
files: ['test_runner/**/*.html']
```

Following qunit, we find the contrib-jshint configuration. The files parameter defines the files that will be linted:

```
files: ['gruntfile.js', 'src/**/*.js', 'test/**/*.js']
```

Notice that gruntfile.js is in the list of files to lint. This is very good practice and will help ensure that no JavaScript errors are introduced into the gruntfile itself. In the preceding example code, the files to be linted include gruntfile.js, all .js files under the src directory, and all .js files under the test directory.

The last plugin to configure in the sample gruntfile is the watch plugin. The contrib-watch plugin responds to changes in files defined by you and runs additional tasks upon being triggered by the changed file events. In this, we define the files to watch and the tasks to run if a watched file changes:

```
files: ['<%= jshint.files %>'],
tasks: ['jshint', 'qunit']
```

In this case, the files that are defined by the contrib-jshint plugin files parameter will be watched and the contrib-jshint and contrib-qunit tasks will be run if any of these watched files change.

Now that all of the configuration is complete for the sample gruntfile plugins, the next step is to load all of the plugins that we will need. This is done in the lines using the `grunt.loadNpmTasks` method. This is very straightforward and self-explanatory:

```
grunt.loadNpmTasks('grunt-contrib-uglify');
grunt.loadNpmTasks('grunt-contrib-jshint');
grunt.loadNpmTasks('grunt-contrib-qunit');
grunt.loadNpmTasks('grunt-contrib-watch');
grunt.loadNpmTasks('grunt-contrib-concat');
```

The final step in the sample gruntfile is to define the custom tasks. The first custom task is set up to run the unit tests. The task is named 'test' and will run the jshint and qunit tasks using the `grunt test` command:

```
grunt.registerTask('test', ['jshint', 'qunit']);
```

Finally, the second custom task defines the default task for the gruntfile. This is the task that will define the actual automated build process. In the default task, the name is defined as `default` and the tasks that will be run are contrib-jshint, contrib-qunit, contrib-concat, and contrib-uglify. It is important to note that these tasks will be run in the order that they are added to the array of tasks argument to the `registerTask` method:

```
grunt.registerTask('default', ['jshint', 'qunit', 'concat',
'uglify']);
```

The default task can be run using the `grunt` command or custom task name in the `grunt.default` command.

Introducing the Grunt API

Uptil now, we haven't discussed any details of the Grunt **Application Programming Interface (API)**. If the appearance of grunt in or around all of the gruntfile code snippets that we have seen so far has caught your eye, then you are to be congratulated for noticing that grunt is providing some things that we need in order to set up and configure our automated tasks.

Grunt exposes all of its properties and methods via the grunt object. Returning to the wrapper function that was provided as an example in the beginning of the gruntfile. js section, we can see that its anonymous function takes the `grunt` object as its only argument:

```
module.exports = function(grunt) {
  // grunt related code
};
```

It is through the `grunt` object that we can access all of its properties and methods and this is why this wrapper method is required.

A discussion of modules will be useful in order to get a better understanding of how node.js can share items, such as objects, properties, and methods, between files. The `module.exports` is a node.js pattern that allows the code within the function to be encapsulated into a single module of code. This module then can expose its contents in order to export whatever is asked for from the caller. The caller uses `require` to import a module. So what problem does this solve? In Node.js, declarations made within a file have scope to only that file. In order to provide a means to share these items across files, we can create modules that expose their contents and allow us to import them to other files. Imagine that we have an external JavaScript file, sum.js, and within it, we have a function that returns the sum of two numbers provided as arguments:

```
//sum.js
var sumOfTwoNumbers = function (x, y) {
    return x + y;
}
```

Only code within sum.js can call the `sumOfTwoNumbers` method. However, if we create a module, then Node can map from one file directly to another file. This is accomplished with the `require` method. The purpose of require() is to load, or import, a module to the calling file. So, for instance, we could load the sum.js file to a file named calculate.js with the following line of code:

```
//calculate.js
var myModule = require('./sum');
```

This would load our sum.js file as a module; however, sum.js still doesn't expose anything because we need to use the `module.exports` function to expose the contents. In order to do this, we can modify sum.js as follows:

```
//sum.js
var sumOfTwoNumbers = function (x, y) {
    return x + y;
}
module.exports.sumOfTwoNumbers = sumOfTwoNumbers;
```

At this point, we now have a sum module that exposes its `sumOfTwoNumbers` method. We can now use this module to calculate a sum for us in the following manner:

```
//calculate.js
var myModule = require('./sum');
var sum = myModule.sumOfTwoNumbers(5, 7);
console.log('The sum of 5 and 7 is: ' + sum);
```

We can test our small node.js application very easily. Create the two files, sum.js and calculate.js, and place them temporarily in the root of the project site. Using the code from the examples, you should have a sum.js file that looks as follows:

```
//sum.js
var sumOfTwoNumbers = function (x, y) {
    return x + y;
}
module.exports.sumOfTwoNumbers = sumOfTwoNumbers;
```

You should also have a calculate.js file that looks like the following:

```
//calculate.js
var myModule = require('./sum');
var sum = myModule.sumOfTwoNumbers(5, 7);
console.log('The sum of 5 and 7 is: ' + sum);
```

Ensure that you are in the root of the sample_project directory:

cd [Your Project Directory]

Now, issue the following command from Terminal in order to run our small node.js program:

```
node calculate.js
```

The output in Terminal should be the content of our `console.log()` method in calculate.js:

```
● ● ●                    🗀 sample_project — bash — 84×29                          ◩
drcsoft-mbp:sample_project dougrdotnet$ node calculate.js
The sum of 5 and 7 is: 12
drcsoft-mbp:sample_project dougrdotnet$ ▌
```

There are other ways to set up `module.exports`; however, the point here is simply to introduce the concept of using `require` to import modules and share code across multiple files. For ECMAScript 6 implementation of modules and module syntax, see the ES6 Module Syntax page at `https://github.com/ModuleLoader/es6-module-loader/wiki/Brief-Overview-of-ES6-Module-syntax`.

Referring to our gruntfile.js, we can now look at the wrapper function with the new understanding that `module.exports` is creating a module of our configuration files. The anonymous function that `module.exports` is set equal to accepts a parameter, grunt. The grunt argument is the `grunt` object whose properties and methods we are using in our configuration, task loading, task registration, and custom task creation. Here are some examples of how we have used the `grunt` object in gruntfile.js thus far.

The wrapper function and initConfig

We will have a better look as wrapper function in this section:

```
module.exports = function(grunt) {
  grunt.initConfig({
        pkg: grunt.file.readJSON('package.json'),
       banner: '/*! <%= pkg.name %>' + ' <%=
    grunt.template.today("yyyy-mm-dd") %> */\n',
      uglify: {
        options: {
            banner: '<%= banner %>'
        },
          ...{
          }
        }
    });
};
```

The `initConfig` method is an alias for the `grunt.config.init` method. The purpose of `grunt.initConfig` is to initialize the grunt configuration object. Within the configuration, we begin with creating a `pkg` object with a value of the contents of package.json. Grunt exposes the grunt.file object's `readJSON` method that takes a parameter of a valid JSON file. The `grunt.template.today` method is a helper function that can be used to obtain and format today's date. Notice the format string that it takes as an argument. The `yyyy-mm-dd` is a format string that will output today's date in the format of the full year, two-digit month, and two-digit date of month.

Loading NPM tasks:

Lets see how to load NPM tasks:

```
grunt.loadNpmTasks('grunt-contrib-uglify');
grunt.loadNpmTasks('grunt-contrib-jshint');
grunt.loadNpmTasks('grunt-contrib-qunit');
grunt.loadNpmTasks('grunt-contrib-watch');
grunt.loadNpmTasks('grunt-contrib-concat');
```

The grunt `loadNPMTasks` method takes an argument of a string name that specifies a locally installed plugin that was installed through NPM.

Creating tasks

The `grunt.registerTask` method registers an alias, `'test'` in this example, with a task list of one or more tasks.

```
grunt.registerTask('test', ['jshint', 'qunit']);
```

Grunt fail API

The `grunt.warn` method will display an error and abort Grunt. There is a flag that can be used in order to warn and continue processing tasks, the `-force` flag. The `grunt.fatal` method will also display an error and abort Grunt.

The Grunt event API

Grunt itself does not dispatch any events; however, the Grunt event API provides the ability to define event listeners and handler methods. Some event methods include the following methods:

- `grunt.event.on(event, listener)`: This adds a listener to the array of listeners for the event defined in the method

- `grunt.event.once(event, listener)`: This adds a one-time-use listener for the specified event, after which time that the event is dispatched, the listener is removed from the array of listeners

- `grunt.event.off(event, listener)`: This method removes an event listener from the array of listeners

- `grunt.event.removeAllListeners([event])`: This removes all listeners from the array of listeners

The Grunt file API

The file API provides methods for file operations, such as reading and writing files and finding files within the filesystem. Grunt leverages many node.js file methods, adding additional options such as logging and error handling.

Reading and writing files are the more common uses of the Grunt File API. The `grunt.file.read`, by default, returns a string representation of the file's contents. In the Grunt template that was used as an example earlier in this chapter, we saw a method, `grunt.file.readJSON`. Like the read method, `readJSON` reads a file and returns a result of JSON formatted data. Another read method is `grunt.file.readYAML`, which does as expected, and returns YAML formatted data.

Grunt provides methods for write operations, including `grunt.file.write`, to write content to files and create directories based on the filepath parameter. The `write` method has a --no-write flag that will prevent write from actually writing the file. This is useful for a test run to ensure that the file writing task behaves as expected. File copy processing is handled by `grunt.file.copy`. The `copy` method takes a source, destination, and option as its arguments and will create directories as needed. Like `file.write`, `file.copy` also has a `--no-write` flag.

Deleting files with recursive deletion of directories is accomplished with the `grunt.file.delete` method. The `file.delete` method will delete the file path specified in its arguments without deleting the current working directory. However, `file.delete` has a --force option that will allow the `file.delete` operation to delete the current directory as well. The `file.delete` method also has a `--no-write` flag.

The directories methods in grunt provide two methods — grunt.file.mkdir creates directories along with any directories needed to be created as provided in the dirpath parameter; file.mkdir command provides a mode parameter that is used to specify directory permissions. If no mode is specified, then the file permissions on a newly created directory will default to 0777 (rwxrwxrwx). The second method is grunt.file.recurse; file.recurse allows recursively accessing directories and executing a callback function for each file contained within. The callback receives the absolute path, root directory, subdirectory, and filename as arguments that can then be used in the callback.

The Grunt file API also includes methods for filename expansion (globbing). Some examples that use expansion are grunt.file.expand, which returns an array of file paths or an array of directory paths. The grunt.file.expandMapping method returns an array of src-dest file mapping objects. The grunt.file.match method returns an array of file paths that match a specified globbing pattern. See the NPM glob project for additional information at https://www.npmjs.com/package/glob. Like the file.match method, grunt.file.isMatch matches files to patterns; however, file.isMatch method returns a Boolean — true, if matching file(s) are found and false, if not.

Additionally, the API provides methods for file type operations such as grunt.file.exists, which checks for the existence of a file, returning a Boolean of a given path result. In order to check whether a given path is a symbolic link, grunt.file.isLink will return a Boolean result. To check for the existence of a directory, grunt.file.isDir will return a Boolean given a specified path. Similarly, in order to determine if a specified path is a file, grunt.file.isFile will provide a Boolean result.

The last section of the Grunt file API is methods for path operations. The grunt.file.isPathAbsolute method returns a Boolean result of whether the given path is an absolute path. To check whether more than one path refers to the same path, grunt.file.arePathsEquivalent will return a Boolean. The grunt.file.doesPathContain method returns a Boolean whether a path's descendants are contained within a specified ancestor path.

The Grunt log API

The main purpose of the grunt.log API is to output messages to the console. The `grunt.log.write` flag creates a log of a string taken as a msg argument. If you wish to write a log with line breaks, `grunt.log.writeLn` adds a trailing new line character to the end of the msg argument. In order to log a msg as an error, the `grunt.log.error` method should be used. If the msg is null, red ERROR text will be logged; otherwise, the error message will be logged with a new line character added to its end. Formatting an error message to 80 columns of text is achieved with the `grunt.log.errorLns` method. To log an OK message in green, use the `grunt.log.ok` method with a null msg argument; otherwise, it will log the message with a trailing new line character. To wrap an OK message to an 80-column format, use the `grunt.log.okLns` method. Bold text can be added to a log message using `grunt.log.subhead`. This will also add a new line character to the end of the message. Logging object properties can be accomplished with the `grunt.log.writeFlags` method. The `log.writeFlags` is useful for debugging, as is `grunt.log.debug`, which logs a debug message only if the `--debug` flag is used.

The Grunt log API has some utility methods that provide a string result that can be used by other methods, not actually generating log entries themselves. For instance, `grunt.log.wordlist` returns an array of comma-separated items. The separator can be defined in options and can also take a color option to color the separator. In order to remove all color from a result, `grunt.log.uncolor` will remove all color information from a string. In order to wrap text at a certain number of characters, the `grunt.log.wraptext` method should be used. Should a table format of text-aligned to columns be desired, `grunt.log.table` will generate output in columns.

The Grunt option API

We have actually seen the Grunt options API being used already. In the configuration section of the sample gruntfile.js earlier, we saw the options being defined for the tasks that we were configuring. For instance, in our pseudo-configuration we saw the following use of options:

```
uglify: {
  options: {
        banner: '<%= banner %>'
  },
    ...{
    }
}
```

The options API provides tasks with a means to share parameters and access command-line flags, such as the --debug flag that was mentioned with the `grunt.log.debug` method. The `grunt.option` simply gets or sets an option. It takes a key, such as `debug`, and a value, such as `true`, which can then be used to determine if the current task should be run in debug mode. The `grunt.option.init` initializes an option and `grunt.option.flags` returns an array of command-line parameters.

Grunt Template API

In the sample gruntfile.js found earlier in this chapter, we saw some examples of templates being used. Recall that we loaded the contents of package.json in an object named `pkg` and then were able to refer to the properties in the `pkg` object through dot notation:

```
dest: 'dist/<%= pkg.name %>.js'
```

In this snippet, we are referring to the name property of the pkg object with `pkg.name`. Notice the `<%=` and `%>` that surround `pkg.name`. These characters are template delimiters and allow the string representation of the value of the template within to be expanded when it is used. The `grunt.template.process` processes Lo-Dash template strings. Discussion of Lo-Dash is out of the scope of this book's purpose; more information on Lo-Dash can be found at `https://lodash.com/docs/#template`. The delimiters shown are the default template delimiters; however, these can be changed with `template.process` using `options.delimiters` to set a custom delimiter. The `template.process` uses `grunt.template.setDelimiters` internally to set delimiters, and `template.setDelimiters` can be used on its own to set custom delimiters too, but it is most commonly achieved with `template.process`.

It should be noted that the grunt object is exposed within a template, so all of the grunt properties and methods are available inside the template delimiters. A simple example would be setting the formatted date using the `grunt.template.today` method as we saw previously when creating a banner string that was used in the contrib-uglify configuration:

```
banner: '/*! <%= pkg.name %>' + ' <%= grunt.template.today("yyyy-mm-
dd") %> */\n'
```

The Grunt task API

The last Grunt API that we will cover is the Grunt task API. We have already seen the API in use in our sample gruntfile earlier in this chapter. The three main purposes of the Grunt task API are to register, run, and load external tasks.

The grunt.task.registerTask registers either an alias task or task function. If task.registerTask is being used to register an alias task, task.registerTask creates an alias for one or more tasks contained within an array of tasks. In the case that a description and function are provided as arguments to task.registerTask, the function argument will be executed when the task is run. The grunt.task. registerMultiTask registers what is known as a multi-task. A multi-task is a task that will run all of its named targets if no specified target exists, or if the target is specified, then it will run only that particular target.

The grunt.task.require ensures that a required task successfully completes; otherwise, the task that requires it will be failed. This allows a task dependency to be created. The grunt.task.exists checks for the existence of a task and returns a Boolean based on the result. The grunt.task.renameTask provides the ability to rename a task and perhaps override the old task with new behavior in the new task. External tasks are loaded from a specified directory with grunt.task.loadTasks. Similarly, grunt.task.loadNpmTasks loads external tasks that were installed with NPM. Tasks can be queued and run on command. The grunt.task.run will run an array of tasks independently from Grunt running all tasks from the command line. The grunt.task.clearQueue will empty any tasks that are queued, entirely.

Summary

In this chapter, we looked at the installation and configuration of Grunt tasks. Focus was placed on two main files in a Grunt project: package.json and Gruntfile.js. As we discovered, the setup process was recorded in package.json as we installed our tasks. You learned about properties and objects that are contained in package. json and discussed the purpose of these properties. The majority of configuration is accomplished in Gruntfile.js. In this file, we encapsulated everything in a wrapper function so that we could export the contents of the file as a module. The main sections of Gruntfile.js consisted of the wrapper function, configuration, task loading, and task registration/custom task creation. After the discussion of Gruntfile.js details, we went deeper into the Grunt API. In this section, we discussed what the Grunt API is and covered specific methods of the API for different types of purposes, for instance, the log API and task API.

In *Chapter 5, Task Setup in the sample_project Application* we will jump into the actual configuration and building of sample_project. Details about the process of running automated builds and inspecting the results of the build process will be covered as we progress. We will take what has been learned about the setting up and configuration of tasks in this chapter, and apply this knowledge to the process of building, testing, and refinement.

5
Task Setup in the sample_project Application

In the previous chapter, we covered the configuration of Grunt tasks and learned about the configuration files that are required by Grunt and the **Grunt Application Programming Interface** (**API**). In this chapter, we will configure the tasks that will be used in the sample_project application. Taking what has been learned about package.json, Gruntfile.js, and the Grunt API, we will build our own Gruntfile.js configuration and look into the details of running automated builds. As we configure and build the project, we will inspect the results to ensure that our automated tasks are doing the work that is expected:

- Defining the requirements of sample_project
- Discussing the wrapper and configuration

Defining requirements of sample_project

Before beginning any work, it is good practice to go through a planning process in order to determine requirements and develop an understanding of what needs to be done. User stories are an excellent tool that are traditionally used to capture feature expectations in software projects for end users. Additionally, they work very well to define process expectations from the perspective of the developer. The basic format of a user story is as follows: as a `<user role>`, I want `<feature>` so that `<purpose>`. So, for instance, we might say: as a developer, I want automated JS linting so that code quality can be maintained. Each user story is that simple.

An overview of user stories

There may be a hierarchy of user stories that will begin with a master slide, (Presentation slides work very well for user stories.) as follows:

- Automated build user stories:
    - As a developer, I want automated builds to automate repetitive tasks
    - As a developer, I want tasks chained to changes so that defined tasks run automatically when files change
    - As a developer, I want automated JS linting to ensure code quality
    - As a developer, I want automated code minification to improve performance

Creation of requirements with user stories is not a difficult process, and it is one that can be performed upfront as well as during development iterations when additional requirements may be discovered. The key is to create the user stories and have them drive development rather than developing first and documenting later. As LeBlank's Law states, later equals never. Requirements documentation has a way of falling by the wayside if it is not created in the correct order. Additionally, creating requirements documentation following development serves no purpose and development only reaps the benefits of documentation if development is driven by requirements documentation. The following presentation slides, normally developed by a project manager or product manager, provide a documentation set that can then be taken by the developer and implemented in order to meet the specifications.

The slide deck

Lets have a look and learn more about slide deck in this section:

This slide creates the requirement to incorporate the banner option in configuration so that project metadata may be accessed from package.json as well as the Grunt object in order to populate the banner content as specified:

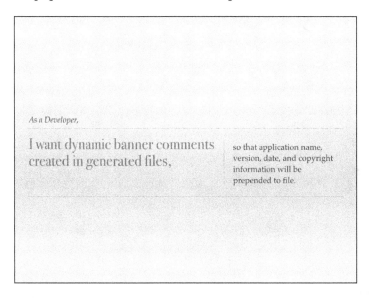

For this story, tasks need to be chained to change events so that other tasks may run automatically when files change. For example, when changes are made to a JavaScript file, we will want the file to be linted automatically. In order to meet this requirement, we will be implementing the contrib-watch plugin:

As alluded to in the previous slide, we definitely want to lint JavaScript and we want to do this in an automated process. Whenever a JavaScript file changes, we will run the contrib-jshint task, which will lint the JavaScript code and ensure that we are writing clean code:

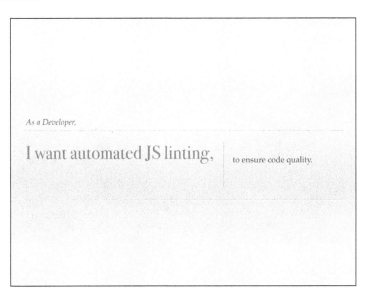

After our JavaScript has successfully passed the linting task, we want to minify the JavaScript and output it to our deployment directory location. The contrib-uglify plugin will satisfy this requirement:

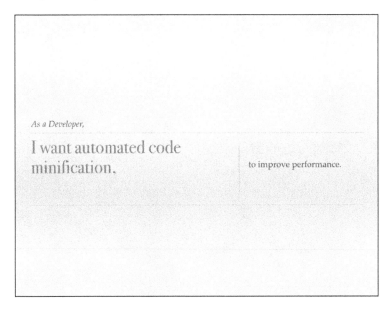

As sample_project will use LESS to provide CSS extensibility, we will want to compile LESS into CSS and place the compiled CSS in the appropriate deployment directory. We will implement the contrib-less task in order to automate our LESS compile process:

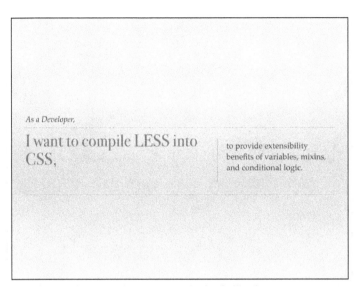

The sample_project will have some images that will need to be optimized before deployment to the web server. In order to facilitate this requirement, we will configure contrib-imagemin to compress the images in the project image directory and output the compressed versions to a distribution deployment directory:

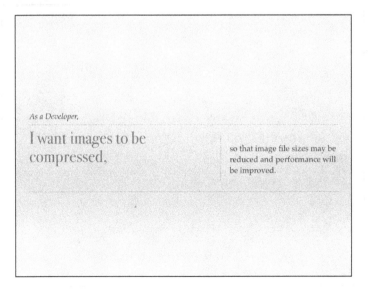

During the automated build process, we will need to receive feedback regarding the success or failure of tasks that are running. While we can get this feedback from Terminal, rather than leaving our IDE, we can configure the grunt-notify task to provide these as automated desktop notifications as OS X Notification Center, Growl, or Windows 8+ Notifications, for example:

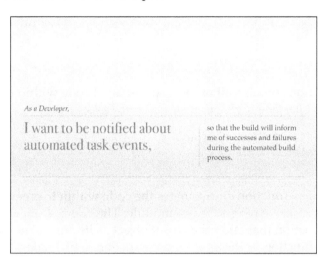

When the automated build successfully completes, this requirement specifies that the application should automatically open in the default browser so that the new changes may be tested. Implementation of the grunt-open task will provide us with this convenience utility so that we can remove some of the repetitive action required to open or refresh our app:

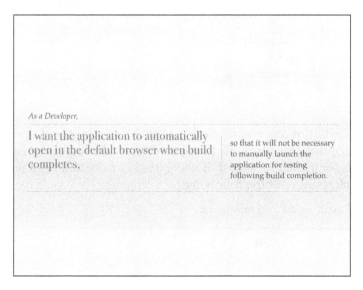

Gruntfile.js wrapper and configuration

Gruntfile.js implements the module pattern that injects the grunt object into its callback function. It is described as a wrapper as it effectively wraps all of the code that will make up the module. Additionally, Gruntfile.js includes all of the configuration for each plugin that is going to be included within. The following sections describe the wrapper and configuration sections of Gruntfile.js.

Wrapper

The wrapper function contains all of the Grunt-related code within its body. Recall the example from *Chapter 4, Configuration of Grunt Tasks*:

```
module.exports = function(grunt) {
  // grunt related code
};
```

The `module.exports` function encapsulates the code within to create an object with properties; in this case, we refer to it as a module. The `module.exports` function is set equal to a function that takes the Grunt object as its argument. Without the `module.exports` function or the anonymous function, which takes the grunt object as a parameter, none of the enclosed code will work. This is required because Grunt uses the `require` function to import the module.

Within the braces of the anonymous function, we will place all of the configuration code that we need in order to configure each task that will be used in sample_project. In order to set up the configuration section of the module, we will need to call on the Grunt object's `initConfig` method to initialize the Grunt configuration object. The Gruntfile.js will start looking something like the following:

```
module.exports = function(grunt) {
  grunt.initConfig({
  // config related code
});
};
```

Tasks will use the Grunt configuration object for their settings and options. As a side note, these options are available to access directly through the `grunt.config.int` method. So, for instance, instead of using `grunt.initConfig`, it is possible to achieve the same result with the following:

```
module.exports = function(grunt) {
  grunt.config.init({
  // config related code
});
};
```

The two previous code examples are equivalent. We will be using the `grunt.initConfig` syntax for sample_project.

grunt-init-gruntfile

In *Chapter 3, All about Grunt Plugins* we mentioned that we could create package.json with a command called grunt-init. In our example, we used the package.json file that was created for us during the Angular-Seed installation. Using the grunt-init utility, we can generate a grunfile.js template automatically with grunt-init-gruntfile. It is perfectly fine to create your Gruntfile.js manually or by means of copy-paste of an example. (See the sample Gruntfile at `http://gruntjs.com/sample-gruntfile`.) Using the grunt-init utility provides us with the convenience of getting started quickly.

First, ensure that grunt-init is currently installed by checking for the current version in **Terminal**:

```
grunt-init -version
```

You should have an output similar to the following:

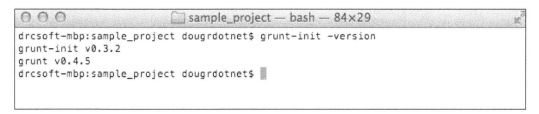

If you do not see a result such as the preceding one, but instead get an error message that indicates that `grunt-init` was not found:

```
-bash: grunt-init: command not found
```

If grunt-init is not installed, then simply run the following install command in order to install grunt-init globally:

```
npm install -g grunt-init
```

Once grunt-init is installed, we can clone the grunt-init-gruntfile utility to the .grunt-init directory, where `~/.grunt-init/` is the path to your .grun-init installation:

```
git clone https://github.com/gruntjs/grunt-init-gruntfile.git ~/.grunt-init/gruntfile
```

The gruntfile utility includes a template to create the Gruntfile.js file. There will be documentation and template located within the newly created gruntfile directory in the `.grunt-init` folder.

Ensure that sample_project is the **Current Working Directory (CWD)**:

```
cd [Your Project Directory]
```

Create a temporary directory in the sample_project root:

```
mkdir temp
```

Make that directory to the CWD:

```
cd temp
```

In the temp directory, we will do a practice run to go through the process of using the gruntfile template generator. At the command line, enter the `grunt-init gruntfile` command to generate Gruntfile.js in the temp directory.

Run the `grunt-init gruntfile` command:

```
grunt-init gruntfile
```

Read the information provided by the task and then proceed through the questions, answering no (n) to each:

```
[?] Is the DOM involved in ANY way? (Y/n)
```

(Select n and press *Enter*)

```
[?] Will files be concatenated or minified? (Y/n)
```

(Select n and press *Enter*)

```
[?] Will you have a package.json file? (Y/n)
```

(Select n and press *Enter*)

```
[?] Do you need to make any changes to the above before continuing? (y/N)
```

(Select N and press *Enter*)

Once the prompt questions have been completed, you should have an output similar to the following:

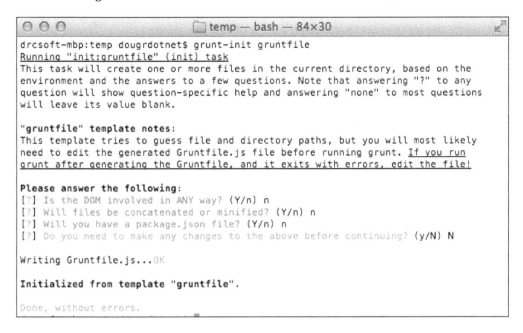

At this time, a gruntfile template has been created for you in the temp directory in the root of your sample_project:

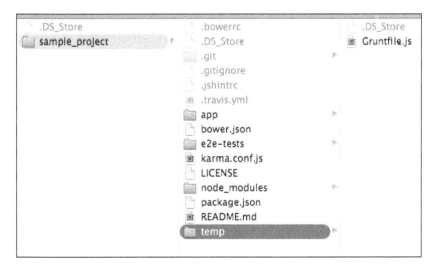

Move Gruntfile.js from temp to the root of sample_project:

```
mv Gruntfile.js ../
```

Then delete the temp directory from the root of sample_project:

```
cd ../
rm -rf temp/
```

Gruntfile.js configuration

This is one way to create Gruntfile.js; alternatively, we can copy and paste the sample Gruntfile from `http://gruntjs.com/sample-gruntfile` or we can start from scratch. We will begin from scratch so that the process of creating Gruntfile.js can be reviewed and discussed as we apply the configuration in the context of sample_project. When completed, we will have a configuration file that is ready to be used to build our project, which we will discuss in the next chapter.

When starting from scratch, first create an empty file in the root of sample_project named Gruntfile.js. Your project tree should look like the following:

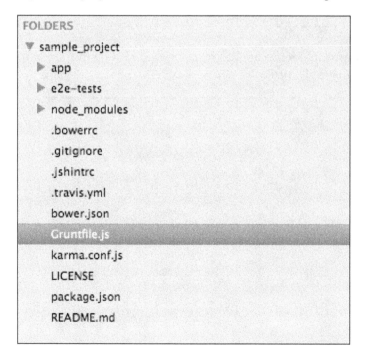

We start with creating the wrapper, which—as discussed—is required in order to inject the Grunt object into the configuration. This is accomplished by the Grunt argument in the anonymous function that is assigned to `module.exports`. The `module.exports` function allows the Grunt configuration to be required as a module by Grunt. This allows the module to be imported by Grunt:

```
Gruntfile.js
1  module.exports = function(grunt) {
2
3
4  };
5
```

Next, we will call on the Grunt object's `initConfig` method in order to initialize the Grunt configuration object. This method will contain our task configuration code whose properties will be used by the plugins. For now, we will just create the method signature and then discuss its contents:

```
Gruntfile.js
1  module.exports = function(grunt) {
2
3    grunt.initConfig({
4
5    });
6
```

Now, referring to the user stories, let's use the list of options and plugins to be implemented as a reference for configuration:

- banner option
- contrib-jshint
- contrib-uglify
- contrib-less
- contrib-imagemin
- notify
- open
- contrib-watch

Beginning with the banner option, we will create the configuration for a banner that can be used for comment headers for generated files, such as in contrib-uglify plugin. The first requirement will be reading the JSON from package.json so that we can use metadata from the file within the banner. We will use Grunt's file class' readJSON method in order to get these contents for us:

```
Gruntfile.js — Documents/.../sample_project

1  module.exports = function(grunt) {
2
3    grunt.initConfig({
4      pkg: grunt.file.readJSON('package.json')
5    });
6
```

The `readJSON` method takes a string argument of the path to package.json and imports the metadata to the Grunt configuration. Once imported, we can use template strings in order to access the configuration properties. In this case, we can access these properties through the pkg object, for example, `<%= pkg.name %>`.

With the package metadata imported to gruntfile, creating the banner with information from package.json is now possible. At this time, some modifications to package.json need to be made to remove some of the boilerplate and add project-specific information, such as the actual project name, author name, and repository location. The top section of metadata in package.json will now look as follows:

```
"name": "sample_project",
  "private": true,
  "version": "0.0.1",
  "description": "Learning Grunt",
  "repository": "https://myrepository.dr-int/project/sample_project",
  "author": {
    "name": "Douglas Reynolds"
  },
```

These changes will support the banner comment content that we wish to include in the head of our generated JavaScript file(s). We can now implement this banner code in Gruntfile.js by accessing the properties of the pkg object, as follows:

```
Gruntfile.js        •    package.json         ×
1   module.exports = function(grunt) {
2
3       grunt.initConfig({
4           // Metadata.
5           pkg: grunt.file.readJSON('package.json'),
6           banner: '/*! *** DO NOT EDIT THIS FILE ***\n' +
7           'It is automatically generated in the build \n' +
8           '<%= pkg.name %> - v<%= pkg.version %> - ' +
9               '<%= grunt.template.today("yyyy-mm-dd") %>\n' +
10              '<%= pkg.repository %>\n' +
11              '* Copyright (c) <%= grunt.template.today("yyyy") %> <%= pkg.author.name %>;*/\n',
12      });
13
```

What we end up with for the banner in this example is text that will provide a message to developers not to modify this file directly. It will provide the name of the application and version along with the date that the file was generated on, location of the repository, and copyright information. Here is an example of what might actually be the output to a file:

```
/*! *** DO NOT EDIT THIS FILE ***

It is automatically generated in the build

gruntTest - v0.0.1 - 2015-11-01

https://myrepository.dr-int/project

Copyright (c) 2015 Douglas Reynolds;*/
```

This completes the banner configuration; the entire Gruntfile.js should now include the following code:

```
module.exports = function(grunt) {
  grunt.initConfig({
    // Metadata.
    pkg: grunt.file.readJSON('package.json'),
    banner: '/*! *** DO NOT EDIT THIS FILE ***\n' +
    'It is automatically generated in the build \n' +
    '<%= pkg.name %> - v<%= pkg.version %> - ' +
      '<%= grunt.template.today("yyyy-mm-dd") %>\n' +
      '<%= pkg.repository %>\n' +
      '* Copyright (c) <%= grunt.template.today("yyyy") %> <%= pkg.
author.name %>;*/\n',
    });
  };
```

Now it is time to begin the configuration of our first task, contrib-jshint. If you recall, the contrib-jshint task will lint the JavaScript to automate the process of checking for errors in the code. We will want contrib-jshint to lint any JavaScript file in our application, and we will use a special file named .jshintrc to specify some options that will be used by jshint. The contrib-jshint plugin may be configured to use its default options by simply not declaring any options. The following example will show you how contrib-jshint may be tailored to specific linting requirements. First, let's have a look at .jshintrc. Save a file in the root of sample_project named .jshintrc, and then add the following JSON formatted options to the file:

```
{
    "curly": true,
    "eqeqeq": true,
    "latedef": true,
    "noarg": true,
    "undef": true,
    "unused": true,
    "boss": true,
    "eqnull": true,
    "node": true
}
```

There are two basic types of options that can be configured for jshint: enforcing and relaxing. Enforcing options will produce errors and/or warning messages, whereas relaxing will suppress warnings.

- curly: This enforces that curly braces are used around blocks in loops and conditions rather than allowing the omission of braces in some cases.

- eqeqeq: This enforces === and !== as opposed to using == or != syntax.

- latedef: This will ensure that variables are not used prior to their definition. noarg prohibits arguments.caller and arguments.callee, which are deprecated in future versions of JavaScript.

- undef: This enforces that all the variables be explicitly declared. unused warns about the variables that are defined but then never used.

- boss: This is a relaxing option that suppresses warnings about assignments where comparisons are expected.

- eqnull: This is a relaxing option that suppresses warnings about the == null comparisons. node is used to define global variables in applications that are running inside of the node environment, such as Grunt in the case of sample_project.

For more information on jshint, refer to the NPM jshint documentation at `https://www.npmjs.com/package/jshint`. Note that in the .jshintrc project, there were also a series of options created by the Angular Seed project scaffolding. These are not discussed here as they are being used by the framework.

Our configuration in Gruntfile.js for contrib-jshint is simply to provide a list of source files that should be linted, any options that should be included, such as `.jshintrc`, and the inclusion of linting Gruntfile.js, as this too is a JavaScript file and we want to ensure that there are no coding errors in our configuration file. Our current contrib-jshint configuration will look like the following:

```
// Task configuration.
jshint: {
  files: ['scripts/main.js'],
  gruntfile: {
    options: {
      jshintrc: '.jshintrc'
    },
    src: 'Gruntfile.js'
  }
}
```

The file's configuration defines the path of an array of files that will be linted. The `gruntfile` specifies the options to be used; in this case, these are located in `.jshintrc`. The `options` may be omitted in order to use jshint's default options, or rather than using the `.jshintrc` file, the `options` may be specified as a JSON formatted list. Finally, the source path of this gruntfile is defined so that Gruntfile.js will be included in the linting.

The contrib-uglify plugin is the next task that we will configure. Recall that contrib-uglify plugin is a code minimizer that will compress our code and output the minimized code to our deployment location. It will use our banner in its output as well as our pkg object to dynamically generate filenames. Here is the contrib-uglify plugin configuration:

```
uglify: {
options: {
banner: '<%= banner %>'
},
dist: {
src: 'scripts/main.js',
dest: 'build/scripts/<%= pkg.name %>.<%= pkg.version %>.min.js'
},
}
```

The uglify configuration provides you with a definition of options that, in this case, takes our banner. The banner content is called in through the template string notation, `<%= banner %>`, which will then be prepended to the minified file output. The `dist` configuration object specifies the source and destination locations for the files to be minified. The `src` parameter provides the file to be minified, and `dest` creates the path and filename of the distribution file to be generated.

Here is the configuration file that we have written thus far:

```
1   module.exports = function(grunt) {
2
3     grunt.initConfig({
4       // Metadata.
5       pkg: grunt.file.readJSON('package.json'),
6       banner: '/*! *** DO NOT EDIT THIS FILE ***\n' +
7       'It is automatically generated in the build \n' +
8       '<%= pkg.name %> - v<%= pkg.version %> - ' +
9         '<%= grunt.template.today("yyyy-mm-dd") %>\n' +
10        '<%= pkg.repository %>\n' +
11        '* Copyright (c) <%= grunt.template.today("yyyy") %> <%= pkg.author.name %>;*/\n',
12      // Task configuration.
13      jshint: {
14        files: ['scripts/main.js'],
15        gruntfile: {
16          options: {
17            jshintrc: '.jshintrc'
18          },
19          src: 'Gruntfile.js'
20        }
21      },
22      uglify: {
23        options: {
24          banner: '<%= banner %>'
25        },
26        dist: {
27          src: 'scripts/main.js',
28          dest: 'build/scripts/<%= pkg.name %>.<%= pkg.version %>.min.js'
29        },
30      }
31    });
32  };
33
```

The next plugin to configure is contrib-less, which will compile LESS into CSS and place the compiled CSS in the appropriate deployment directory. By now, the pattern of configuration should be evident. Each task configuration is different; however, the general format of each is quite similar. Here is the contrib-less configuration code for us to discuss:

```
less: {
  options: {
    paths: ["styles"]
  },
  dist: {
    src: 'styles/main.less',
```

```
      dest: 'styles/main.css'
    }
  }
}
```

First, an options object is defined with a paths property that defines the directory name that contrib-less will scan for `@import` directives (normally the same directory as the source file location). Next, the dist object defines the src and destination paths to be used to create the CSS distribution file. The contrib-less plugin will compile the file in the source directory into CSS and write the new file to the distribution location. If there are any `@import` directives, contrib-less will include these in the compilation.

Next in line is contrib-imagemin, which will be used for the minification of images. This process will compress the images in the project's image source directory and output the compressed versions to a distribution deployment directory. The contrib-imagemin plugin has not yet been installed in the project; we can use this as a quick review on installing a plugin with **Node Package Manager** (**NPM**). Installation of contrib-imagemin is accomplished with the same `npm install` command:

`npm install grunt-contrib-imagemin --save-dev`

After running the installation command, contrib-imagemin will be installed in the node-modules directory located at the root of sample_project. Additionally, the plugin will be registered in package.json devDependencies with a line that will resemble `grunt-contrib-imagemin": "^0.9.4`. At this point, we can go forward with the configuration in Gruntfile.js:

```
imagemin: {
  dynamic: {
    files: [{
      expand: true,
      cwd: 'images/',
      src: ['**/*.{png,jpg,gif}'],
      dest: 'dist/'
    }]
  }
}
```

Imagemin provides you with two types of target configurations: static and dynamic. In a static configuration, each file and destination is listed specifically, such as images/img.png: dist/img.png. In this example, the path and filename of source and destination are explicit. In the preceding code example, a dynamic target is being configured. Notice that a dynamic target is specified that contains the file's configuration. Expand is set to true, which will enable dynamic expansion, and cwd is the source path relative to the CWD. Notice that src is configured to use wildcards.

The path wildcard, **/*.{png,jpg,gif}, is of interest, which reads as follows: match any number of characters (**/), including (/), and then match any number of characters (*) (.) match png, jpg, or gif file extensions. Using this matching syntax, we can traverse the images directory for any image name that is of a png, jpg, or gif type. Finally, the destination location is defined as the dist directory. It is recommended to use the grunt-newer plugin with contrib-imagemin, which can be configured to run only contrib-imagemin on files that have changed. This helps reduce unnecessary minification time wasted on images that have not changed since last being compressed. Have a look at the NPM grunt-newer plugin documentation for more information at https://www.npmjs.com/package/grunt-newer.

The notify is the next plugin to be configured and is really one of the coolest plugins. Getting notifications on the status is convenient and keeps a developer from having to leave their IDE to go look at the Terminal output. With notify, we can provide feedback with automated desktop notifications in OS X Notification Center, Growl, or Windows 8+ Notifications, for example. We have not yet installed notify in sample_project, so, as usual, run the NPM installation command on notify:

```
npm install grunt-notify –save-dev
```

This installs notify in the node-modules directory and adds an entry to devDependencies, which will look similar to grunt-notify": "^0.4.1. The notify configuration will include each plugin that you wish to receive a notification of the status of success or failure along with a custom title and message for success. In failure, the notification will include the error or warning message. The sample_project configuration will look as follows:

```
notify: {
   jshint: {
 options: {
            title: 'Linting Complete',
            message: 'jshint finished',
        }
   },
   uglify: {
 options: {
            title: 'Minification Complete',
```

```
            message: 'javascript is minified'
        }
    },
    less: {
options: {
            title: 'LESS Compiled',
            message: 'CSS is generated'
        }
    },
    imagemin: {
options: {
            title: 'Images Minified',
            message: 'Images are minified'
        }
    }
}
```

In sample_project, there will be notifications for tasks to include contrib-jshint, contrib-uglify, contrib-less, and contrib-imagemin. The configuration includes a block for each plugin to be configured with notifications. Within each block is an options object with title and message properties. Title is optional and message is required. This configuration will set up notifications for each of the defined tasks and then present the build status notification for each task.

When the build has completed successfully, it will be convenient for the application to open, refreshed with changes, in the default browser. To begin, we need to install grunt-open using NPM:

```
npm install grunt-open --save-dev
```

The open can be found in the node-modules directory and will be registered in package.json devDependencies, similar to `grunt-open": "^0.2.3`. Once installed, configuration is straightforward with the following implementation:

```
open : {
  dev : {
    path: 'http://localhost:8000/app/index.html',
    app: 'Google Chrome'
  }
}
```

In this example, open is configured with a dev environment object that contains path and app properties. Multiple environment configurations can be contained within open, for instance, dev, test, and prod environments can be configured to meet your requirements. In this case, we will configure a single development environment to open our application in our local node HTTP server that is running on localhost port 8000 with a path to index.html: http://localhost:8000/app/index.html. Additionally, Google Chrome is used as the browser to open and run the sample_project application. When run, Google Chrome will be launched and the changes will be updated for the testing.

Finally, we will configure contrib-watch. As this has already been installed, we can go right into the configuration. Recall first that watch chains tasks to change events so that other tasks may run automatically when files change. The contrib-watch plugin is key for us to fully automate the build process; otherwise, each time we wish to build, we would need to go to the Terminal window and run the Grunt command to kick off the build process. Configuration of watch is typical, as shown here in the implementation:

```
watch: {
    gruntfile: {
        files: 'Gruntfile.js',
        tasks: ['jshint','uglify','less','imagemin'],
    },
    scripts: {
        files:['scripts/*.js','styles/*.less'],
        tasks: ['default']
    }
}
```

The watch task has two objects specified to watch in this configuration. The first is to look for changes in Gruntfile.js itself. In the case of sample_project, contrib_watch is configured to run contrib-jshint, contrib-uglify, contrib-less, and contrib-imagemin if Gruntfile.js changes. As seen in the configuration, the files property defines which file(s) to watch and the tasks property defines which tasks to run when the specified file(s) change. In the second half of the configuration, we are setting up a scripts watch that will watch any files with .js extensions that exist in the scripts directory as well as files that have the .less extension located in the styles directory. When any of these files change, watch will run the default task, which we will look at in the next chapter.

At this point, our Gruntfile.js configuration should look like the following:

```
module.exports = function(grunt) {
    'use strict';
    grunt.initConfig({
```

```
    // Metadata.
    pkg: grunt.file.readJSON('package.json'),
    banner: '/*! *** DO NOT EDIT THIS FILE ***\n' +
    'It is automatically generated in the build \n' +
    '<%= pkg.name %> - v<%= pkg.version %> - ' +
      '<%= grunt.template.today("yyyy-mm-dd") %>\n' +
      '<%= pkg.repository %>\n' +
      '* Copyright (c) <%= grunt.template.today("yyyy") %> <%= pkg.
author.name %>;*/\n',
    // Task configuration.
    jshint: {
      files: ['scripts/main.js'],
      gruntfile: {
        options: {
          jshintrc: '.jshintrc'
        },
        src: 'Gruntfile.js'
      }
    },
    uglify: {
      options: {
        banner: '<%= banner %>'
      },
      dist: {
        src: 'scripts/main.js',
        dest: 'build/scripts/<%= pkg.name %>.<%= pkg.version %>.min.
js'
      },
    },
    less: {
      options: {
        paths: ["styles"]
      },
      dist: {
        src: 'styles/main.less',
        dest: 'styles/main.css'
      }
    },
    imagemin: {
      dynamic: {
        files: [{
          expand: true,
          cwd: 'images/',
          src: ['**/*.{png,jpg,gif}'],
```

```
          dest: 'dist/'
        }]
      }
    },
    notify: {
      jshint: {
        options: {
          title: 'Linting Complete',
          message: 'jshint finished',
        }
      },
      uglify: {
        options: {
          title: 'Minification Complete',
          message: 'javascript is minified'
        }
      },
      less: {
        options: {
          title: 'LESS Compiled',
          message: 'CSS is generated'
        }
      },
      imagemin: {
        options: {
          title: 'Images Minified',
          message: 'Images are minified'
        }
      },
      watch: {
        options: {
          title: 'Watch Started',
          message: 'Watch is running'
        }
      }
    },
    open : {
      dev : {
        path: 'http://localhost:8000/app/index.html',
        app: 'Google Chrome'
      }
    },
    watch: {
      gruntfile: {
```

```
          files: 'Gruntfile.js',
          tasks: ['jshint','uglify','less','imagemin'],
        },
        scripts: {
          files:['scripts/*.js','styles/*.less'],
          tasks: ['default']
        }
      },
    });
  };
```

Summary

In this chapter, we discussed defining the sample_project automated build process using user stories to outline specific features that need to be included in the process. We then covered the Gruntfile.js configuration section from top to bottom, discussing the configuration of all the tasks used in sample_project's automated build process along the way. In the next chapter, we will cover task loading and incremental testing as well as defining the custom default task that will govern the entire build process and simplify our launching of the automated build to the need of only a single `grunt` command from Terminal.

6
Building the Sample Project

In this chapter we will discuss the process of final build configuration and then actually running automated builds of the sample_project. We will learn:

- **Loading tasks**: We will have a look at loading tasks to be run, adding them incrementally so we can check the configuration and ensure the expected results are being generated

- **Defining custom and default tasks**: The custom tasks will provide the means to configure custom task functionality for specific situations. The default task will allow us to create a launch configuration. This will require only a single command from the terminal to start up our automated build.

- **Functional testing**: Functional testing will provide examples of how to run and check the specific outcomes of each of the tasks included in our automated build

Understanding task loading

The process and syntax for loading a task are quite simple and very straightforward. In fact, the basic way to load a task is a simple one-liner using Grunt's loadNpmTasks method.

The syntax is:

```
grunt.loadNpmTasks('name-of-task');
```

The name-of-task, as shown in the example, would be the name of the task as defined in sample_project's package.json devDependencies object. So, for instance, to load grunt-contrib-uglify we would specify it as the argument in the loadNpmTasks method like this:

```
grunt.loadNpmTasks('grunt-contrib-uglify');
```

Using the LoadNpmTasks method

A little about loadNpmTasks. The loadNpmTasks method is a method that loads plugins installed locally with NPM (it will not load tasks installed via other means) and that have been installed relative to the gruntfile. In order to load tasks not installed with NPM, one would use `grunt.loadTasks`, an alias for `grunt.task.loadTasks`. Additionally, for tasks that have been installed with NPM, one may also use `grunt.task.loadNpmTasks`. The alias makes them synonymous. The syntax difference lies in the synonyms:

```
grunt.loadTasks('name-of-task');
```

is the same as:

```
grunt.task.loadTasks('name-of-task');
```

we also have to do:

```
grunt.loadNpmTasks('name-of-task');
```

which is the same as:

```
grunt.task.loadNpmTasks('name-of-task');
```

Calling plugins using the loadNpmTasks method

The following will provide the code for loading each plugin we are using in the sample_project. Note that we installed all of the plugins using NPM, so we will use the loadNpmTasks method for each plugin.

`contrib-jshint` plugin:

```
grunt.loadNpmTasks('grunt-contrib-jshint');
```

`contrib-uglify` plugin:

```
grunt.loadNpmTasks('grunt-contrib-uglify');
```

`contrib-less` plugin:

```
grunt.loadNpmTasks('grunt-contrib-less');
```

`contrib-imagemin` plugin:

```
grunt.loadNpmTasks('grunt-contrib-imagemin');
```

`contrib-notify` plugin:

```
grunt.loadNpmTasks('grunt-notify');
```

`contrib-open` plugin:

```
grunt.loadNpmTasks('grunt-open');
```

`contrib-watch` plugin:

```
grunt.loadNpmTasks('grunt-contrib-watch');
```

For this style of loading, all of the loadNpmTasks calls are placed after the configuration section, as follows:

```
grunt.loadNpmTasks('grunt-contrib-jshint');
grunt.loadNpmTasks('grunt-contrib-uglify');
grunt.loadNpmTasks('grunt-contrib-less');
grunt.loadNpmTasks('grunt-contrib-imagemin');
grunt.loadNpmTasks('grunt-contrib-watch');
grunt.loadNpmTasks('grunt-notify');
grunt.loadNpmTasks('grunt-open');
```

Using the devDependencies object looping method

While this is the way in which Grunt documents the usage of loadNpmTasks, there is a more elegant way. By looping through the `devDependencies` object to get each one of the dependencies defined within, all of the tasks may be loaded without the need to explicitly load each one. This is done simply with the following syntax:

```
Object.keys(require('./package.json').devDependencies).
    forEach(function(dep) {
grunt.loadNpmTasks(dep);
});
```

Let's break this down. `Object` is the object which contains the properties (or, in this case, tasks properties) that we wish to use. We will use the Object's keys method to return only the names of the properties, which will be the tasks listed as dependencies in `devDependencies`. Require includes a defined file and `require(./package.json).devDependencies` returns the `devDependencies` object in package.json, which is then looped over for each property and returned and loaded with `grunt.loadNpmTasks` on each iteration of the loop. Using this approach we could add and remove tasks from package.json and config without having to worry about loading. However, in our case using the Angular-Seed project, there are many tasks in `devDependencies` that we do not need within our automated build process. For this reason it will be better to explicitly load each task.

At this time our Gruntfile.js should look like the following:

```javascript
module.exports = function(grunt) {
  'use strict';
  grunt.initConfig({
    // Metadata.
    pkg: grunt.file.readJSON('package.json'),
    banner: '/*! *** DO NOT EDIT THIS FILE ***\n' +
    'It is automatically generated in the build \n' +
    '<%= pkg.name %> - v<%= pkg.version %> - ' +
      '<%= grunt.template.today("yyyy-mm-dd") %>\n' +
      '<%= pkg.repository %>\n' +
      '* Copyright (c) <%= grunt.template.today("yyyy") %> <%= pkg.
author.name %>;*/\n',
    // Task configuration.
    jshint: {
      files: ['scripts/main.js'],
      gruntfile: {
        options: {
          jshintrc: '.jshintrc'
        },
        src: 'Gruntfile.js'
      }
    },
    uglify: {
      options: {
        banner: '<%= banner %>'
      },
      dist: {
        src: 'scripts/main.js',
        dest: 'build/scripts/<%= pkg.name %>.<%= pkg.version %>.min.
js'
      },
    },
    less: {
      options: {
        paths: ["styles"]
      },
      dist: {
        src: 'styles/main.less',
        dest: 'styles/main.css'
      }
    },
    imagemin: {
      dynamic: {
```

```
      files: [{
        expand: true,
        cwd: 'images/',
        src: ['**/*.{png,jpg,gif}'],
        dest: 'dist/'
      }]
    }
  },
  notify: {
    jshint: {
      options: {
        title: 'Linting Complete',
        message: 'jshint finished',
      }
    },
    uglify: {
      options: {
        title: 'Minification Complete',
        message: 'JavaScript is minified'
      }
    },
    less: {
      options: {
        title: 'LESS Compiled',
        message: 'CSS is generated'
      }
    },
    imagemin: {
      options: {
        title: 'Images Minified',
        message: 'Images are minified'
      }
    },
    watch: {
      options: {
        title: 'Watch Started',
        message: 'Watch is running'
      }
    }
  },
  open : {
    dev : {
      path: 'http://localhost:8000/app/index.HTML',
      app: 'Google Chrome'
```

```
      }
    },
    watch: {
      gruntfile: {
        files: 'Gruntfile.js',
        tasks: ['jshint','uglify','less','imagemin'],
      },
      scripts: {
        files:['scripts/*.js','styles/*.less'],
        tasks: ['default']
      }
    },
  });

  grunt.loadNpmTasks('grunt-contrib-jshint');
  grunt.loadNpmTasks('grunt-contrib-uglify');
  grunt.loadNpmTasks('grunt-contrib-less');
  grunt.loadNpmTasks('grunt-contrib-imagemin');
  grunt.loadNpmTasks('grunt-contrib-watch');
  grunt.loadNpmTasks('grunt-notify');
  grunt.loadNpmTasks('grunt-open');
};
```

We have just one more item to add in order to complete our automated build. This is to create our custom and default tasks. While sample_project won't use a custom task, per se, an example of what this is and why we might want to use one or more custom tasks will be discussed in the next section.

The default task configuration

Creating the default task is as simple as loading tasks. Grunt has a `registerTask` method that we use to name (alias) the task and provide a list of one or more tasks to be run. When the task alias is run, all of the associated tasks in its list are run. In this way we can create a single command that runs the task(s) in the associated list. Additionally, the order of the tasks in the list defines the order in which the tasks are run; this provides us with even more refined control.

The basic task configuration syntax is:

```
grunt.registerTask(task_name, task_list);
```

In order to define the default task, the task name given should be 'default'. This task will run all of the associated tasks in its list even if no tasks are specified. For example, in order to run the default task, all that is needed is to issue the `grunt` command in the command prompt. The list argument to the registerTask method is an array of tasks. This syntax looks like the following example:

```
grunt. registerTask (taskName, [task1, task2, task3, etc...]);
```

So, for instance, our default task for sample_project would be configured like this:

```
grunt.registerTask('default',['jshint','uglify', 'less', 'imagemin',
'notify', 'open', 'watch']);
```

In this example the default task alias is created and the list of the jshint, uglify, less, imagemin, notify, open, and watch tasks will be run in that same order listed. Even if only a single task is specified, it must be contained within an array. Task arguments may be run directly from within the task list as well. For instance, the uglify dist argument could be passed directly by calling the uglify task with the `dist` parameter as follows:

```
grunt.registerTask('default',['uglify:dist']);
```

The default task configuration is added following the task loading so that the tasks are registered prior to attempting to run them. The very last line of our sample_project Gruntfile will be the default task example as provided earlier. This code looks like the following now:

```
101    grunt.loadNpmTasks('grunt-contrib-jshint');
102    grunt.loadNpmTasks('grunt-contrib-uglify');
103    grunt.loadNpmTasks('grunt-contrib-less');
104    grunt.loadNpmTasks('grunt-contrib-imagemin');
105    grunt.loadNpmTasks('grunt-contrib-watch');
106    grunt.loadNpmTasks('grunt-notify');
107    grunt.loadNpmTasks('grunt-open');
108
109    grunt.registerTask('default',['jshint','uglify', 'less', 'imagemin', 'notify', 'open', 'watch']);
```

At this point we are ready to begin functional testing on our Gruntfile, but before we begin that process let's look at creating custom tasks.

A custom task configuration

Custom tasks are just like the default task; however, we can define subsets of tasks or special functionality that we wish to run to provide specific build functionality. For instance, consider the use case of building for a development server versus building for test or production servers. It may not be desirable to have minified code on the development server so that it is easier to debug code. We could define a custom task named dev that will not include any minification of JavaScript or CSS but still provides tasks for linting of JavaScript, compiling LESS, compressing images, and so on. An example custom task might look like the following:

```
grunt.registerTask('dev',['jshint','less', 'imagemin', 'notify',
'open', 'watch']);
```

If you wish, you can add a function callback to your custom task to add additional logic or run other tasks. For example, we could write the preceding custom task with the following syntax:

```
grunt.registerTask('dev', 'description of dev task', function() {
    grunt.task.run(['jshint', 'less', 'imagemin', 'notify', 'open',
'watch']);
});
```

A custom task callback may also take arguments so that you could pass in task names to be run as needed from the command line, for example. If running jshint, less, and open were the only tasks needed for a particular local development process, a task could be created like this:

```
grunt.registerTask('local', 'description of local task', function(a,
b, c) {
    grunt.task.run([a, b, c]);
});
```

You could then enter the following command at the command prompt to launch your set of tasks:

```
grunt local:jshint:uglify:less
```

The result of running this custom task would look similar to this screenshot:

```
drcsoft-mbp:gruntTest dougrdotnet$ grunt local:jshint:uglify:less
Running "local:jshint:uglify:less" (local) task

Running "jshint:files" (jshint) task
>> 1 file lint free.

Running "jshint:gruntfile" (jshint) task
>> 1 file lint free.

Running "uglify:dist" (uglify) task
File "build/scripts/gruntTest.0.0.1.min.js" created.

Running "less:dist" (less) task
File styles/main.css created.

Done, without errors.
```

Custom tasks can be taken further to add custom logic and functionality. We will have a look at a more advanced custom task in the next chapter.

Functional testing

We have reached a point in our sample_project Gruntfile setup where we are ready to begin testing the functionality of each registered task to ensure that we are meeting the project requirements. Recall that we have implemented the following plugins:

- contrib-jshint
- contrib-uglify
- contrib-less
- contrib-imagemin
- notify
- open
- contrib-watch

Starting at the top, we will test each requirement individually, then we will begin adding in the entire stack to create our automated build process. We do have a banner option that is not a task; it is simply a property with a value that we can use elsewhere. In the case of our configuration, the banner is used by contrib-uglify. We will start with contrib-jshint testing.

The process for testing individual tasks is simple: we will only register the task we wish to test and then inspect the result of the task to ensure that what we expected to happen has indeed happened. Our custom task with a callback function that takes arguments is a handy way to test each task; we will set that up now so that we can call each task independently.

```
grunt.registerTask('testing', 'testing individual tasks', function(a)
{
  grunt.task.run([a]);
});
```

As you can see, our custom register task method will take a single argument that will be the task we wish to run, then the callback will run that task for us. The terminal syntax for testing each plugin configuration will be the same, the only difference being the name of the plugin that gets passed in to the callback function. For each plugin the syntax will be as follows:

```
grunt testing:plugin-name
```

We will then inspect the resulting output; for instance, with contrib-jshint we will ensure that it runs and detects errors. For contrib-uglify we will inspect the output file contents to ensure that the banner was created correctly and that our JavaScript code was minified. We will continue through all of the plugins in this fashion.

Testing the contrib-jshint configuration

First, let's make a small change to the path of the file parameter of the jshint configuration. We want to check that our JavaScript files are lint-free and we will start by adding app.js to the files to lint. The path change will point to our app directory where app.js resides:

```
jshint: {
  files: ['app/app.js'],
  gruntfile: {
    options: {
        jshintrc: '.jshintrc'
    },
    src: 'Gruntfile.js'
  }
},
```

Let's do a preliminary run of jshint. There may be some errors and warnings that we will need to debug until jshint is lint free. Ensure you are in the correct directory location in Terminal and change directories if needed to the root of sample_project:

```
cd path/to/sample_project/
```

Then, using the syntax illustrated earlier, run the jshint task:

```
grunt testing:jshint
```

Immediately, there are errors and warnings that will need to be addressed. The following output is telling us that use strict should be wrapped inside the function instead of being used outside the function scope. In this case it is pointing to the use strict that is found at the head of our app.js file.

Here is the output:

```
Running "testing:jshint" (testing) task

Running "jshint:files" (jshint) task

   app/app.js
      1 |'use strict';
          ^ Use the function form of "use strict".
      4 |angular.module('myApp', [
          ^ 'angular' is not defined.

>> 2 errors in 1 file
Warning: Task "jshint:files" failed. Use --force to continue.

Aborted due to warnings.
```

Since we know that we will not have any issues with use strict in Gruntfile.js or app.js, we can safely suppress the error by adding the .jshintrc option to the main body of the jshint configuration like this:

```
jshint: {
      files: ['app/app.js'],
      options: {
          jshintrc: '.jshintrc'
      },
      gruntfile: {
        options: {
          jshintrc: '.jshintrc'
        },
        src: 'Gruntfile.js'
      }
   },
```

The reason this will work is because, if you notice, we already provide a jshintrc option to the gruntfile property, which also has use strict at the head of the file. Looking at the .jshintrc file, which if you recall is used to define jshint options, there is a line which suppresses strict error messages:

```
"strict": false,
```

Now, run the jshint task again and check the output. Notice that the use strict error is no longer present in the lint message. We can clean up the jshint a bit now because we no longer need the gruntfile option for jshintrc, given that we added the jshintrc option to the main body of the jshint configuration.

Remove the gruntfile jshintrc option:

```
jshint: {
        files: ['app/app.js'],
        options: {
            jshintrc: '.jshintrc'
        },
        gruntfile: {
          src: 'Gruntfile.js'
        }
    },
```

The jshint class runs without errors since they are suppressed by the configuration in jshintrc.

```
Running "testing:jshint" (testing) task

Running "jshint:files" (jshint) task
>> 1 file lint free.

Running "jshint:gruntfile" (jshint) task
>> 1 file lint free.

Done, without errors.
```

The final step is to add to the path array, any additional files that should be linted. In the case of sample_app, these are located in the app/view1 and app/view2 directories:

```
jshint: {
    files: ['app/app.js', 'app/view1/*.js', 'app/view2/*.js'],
    options: {
        jshintrc: '.jshintrc'
    },
    gruntfile: {
```

```
        src: 'Gruntfile.js'
    }
  },
```

As is illustrated by the `files` configuration, the use of wildcards is a perfectly acceptable and efficient way to include files in the configuration.

In this case, there will be a total of five files plus the gruntfile linted that completes our functional testing of jshint:

```
drcsoft-mbp:sample_project dougrdotnet$ grunt
Running "jshint:files" (jshint) task
>> 5 files lint free.

Running "jshint:gruntfile" (jshint) task
>> 1 file lint free.

Done, without errors.
```

Testing the contrib-uglify configuration

For the purposes of illustrating the configuration of contrib-uglify, let's say that we need our JavaScript files in a `scripts` directory that the HTML files will use on the Test and Production servers. The contrib-uglify plugin will minify our development JavaScript and put it in our distribution location: `dist/scripts`. Then for production, the related HTML files would be modified to use the relative links to the minified JavaScript files in the dist/scripts directory. Don't worry about creating any directories; when we configure uglify to use the dist/scripts path, it will be created for us automatically if it does not already exist.

The first thing to do is modify the uglify configuration with the new directory paths, and set up dynamic naming for our generated, minified, JavaScript file:

```
uglify: {
    options: {
       banner: '<%= banner %>'
    },
    dist: {
       src: ['app/app.js', 'app/view1/view1.js', 'app/view2/view2.js'],
       dest: 'dist/scripts/<%= pkg.name %>.<%= pkg.version %>.min.js'
    },
  },
```

In the `dist` configuration the `src` property is changed to an array of source files to be minified. The three sample_project JavaScript files of interest are app.js, view1. js, and view2.js. These three files will be minified and concatenated together into a file created and named dynamically using properties from package.json, via our pkg variable. Additionally, the banner we created previously will be prepended to the minified file.

Run the uglify task:

```
grunt testing:uglify
```

```
drcsoft-mbp:sample_project dougrdotnet$ grunt testing:uglify
Running "testing:uglify" (testing) task

Running "uglify:dist" (uglify) task
>> 1 file created.

Done, without errors.
```

Now have a look at the file tree to see the new destination directory and minified file that were created:

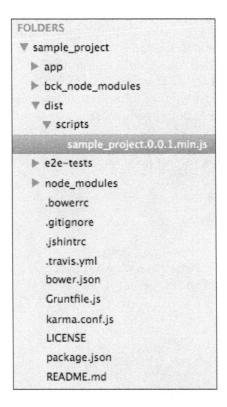

Modify sample_project's `index.html` to point to the new minified JavaScript file and comment out the imports for the three source files:

```
34    <script src="bower_components/angular/angular.js"></script>
35    <script src="bower_components/angular-route/angular-route.js"></script>
36    <script src="../../dist/scripts/sample_project.0.0.1.min.js"></script>
37    <!--script src="view1/view1.js"></script>
38    <script src="view2/view2.js"></script-->
39    <script src="components/version/version.js"></script>
40    <script src="components/version/version-directive.js"></script>
41    <script src="components/version/interpolate-filter.js"></script>
```

Navigate to `http://localhost:8000/app/#/view1` and test the application.

Have a look at the minified JavaScript file, `sample_project.0.0.1.min.js`, located in the `dist/scripts` directory. Notice that the banner has been prepended and the three files have been minified and concatenated together:

```
/*! *** DO NOT EDIT THIS FILE ***
It is automatically generated in the build
sample_project - v0.0.1 - 2015-12-29
https://myrepository.dr-int/project/sample_project
* Copyright (c) 2015 Douglas Reynolds;*/
"use strict";angular.module("myApp",["ngRoute","myApp.view1","myApp.
view2","myApp.version"]).config(["$routeProvider",function(a)
{a.otherwise({redirectTo:"/view1"})}]),angular.module("myApp.
view1",["ngRoute"]).config(["$routeProvider",function(a){a.when("/
view1",{templateUrl:"view1/view1.HTML",controller:"View1Ctrl"})}]).
controller("View1Ctrl",[function(){}]),angular.module("myApp.
view2",["ngRoute"]).config(["$routeProvider",function(a){a.when("/
view2",{templateUrl:"view2/view2.HTML", controller:"View2Ctrl"})}]).co
ntroller("View2Ctrl",[function(){}]);
```

Testing the contrib-less Configuration

This section assumes a little knowledge about LESS; however, the example will be very simple and I will walk through each line to explain what is going on. Even if you don't use LESS, this is a good example of the power of automated tasks.

The process for configuring and testing contrib-less will be similar to uglify. It will be necessary to modify the existing `app.css` by adding some LESS and renaming the file to `app.less` so that it will be compiled by the LESS processor. A distribution directory will be created with a style directory where the compiled CSS file will be generated. The path will be `dist/styles`.

To begin, rename app.css to change the file extension to .less. When complete the file will be named app.less. Next, add some LESS.

Here is the example that will be used to style the menu:

```less
@blue: #5B83AD;

.box-shadow(@style, @a) {
  -webkit-box-shadow: @style @a;
  box-shadow:         @style @a;
}
.menu {
  @light-blue: (@blue + #111);
  color: saturate(@light-blue, 5%);
  border-color: lighten(@light-blue, 30%);
  .box-shadow(0 0 5px, @blue);
}
```

A quick walk-through is in order. The first line creates a variable for a `blue` color. The `@` designates that it is a variable, `blue` is the variable name, and its value is the hexadecimal color `#5B83AD`.

Next is a mixin `.box-shadow` that takes arguments, much like a function. Because it behaves like a function, we could have many different callers of `.box-shadow` that pass in different values for arguments that will be used within their particular element style.

Finally, we have the `.menu` element style declaration, which creates a new color of light-blue from our base blue color. Then the color style is assigned the light-blue color within the `saturate` method, saturating the color by `5%`. The menu border color is assigned the light-blue color and lightened, using the `lighten` method, by `30%`. The box-shadow mixin is called and arguments passed for the box-shadow style. The style definition for box-shadow is:

```
box-shadow: none|h-shadow v-shadow blur spread color
```

In the example we pass in `h-shadow` of `0`, v-shadow of `0`, blur of `5px`, and the `color`. `Spread` is optional and omitted:

```less
.box-shadow(0 0 5px, @blue);
```

This line is of particular interest because it is here we are calling the mixin and passing in the arguments. The result of the mixin will become the `.box-shadow` style defined within the `.menu` style declaration.

The entire contents of app.less will now look like the following:

```less
@blue: #5B83AD;

.box-shadow(@style, @color) {
  -webkit-box-shadow: @style @color;
  box-shadow:         @style @color;
}
.menu {
  @light-blue: (@blue + #111);
  color: saturate(@light-blue, 5%);
  border-color: lighten(@light-blue, 30%);
  .box-shadow(0 0 5px, #5B83AD);
}

.menu:before {
  content: «[«;
}

.menu:after {
  content: «]»;
}

.menu > li {
  display: inline;
}

.menu > li:before {
  content: "|";
  padding-right: 0.3em;
}

.menu > li:nth-child(1):before {
  content: "";
  padding: 0;
}
```

At this point, it is time to go back to Gruntfile.js and make the necessary modifications to the LESS configuration. First, we will need to set the options paths property to be the directory that contains the input file; in this case, app.less exists with the `app` directory. We will then need to define the dist properties for the source and destination paths. The source is located in `app/app.less` and the destination will be `dist/styles/main.css`.

The LESS configuration section will be as follows:

```
less: {
    options: {
        paths: ["app"]
    },
    dist: {
        src: 'app/app.less',
        dest: 'dist/styles/main.css'
    }
},
```

Once the LESS configuration and app.less have been modified and saved, it is time to run the task to inspect the resulting behavior and generated file:

```
grunt testing:less
```

```
drcsoft-mbp:sample_project dougrdotnet$ grunt testing:less
Running "testing:less" (testing) task

Running "less:dist" (less) task
>> 1 stylesheet created.

Done, without errors.
```

If all has gone well, a new directory, named `styles`, will be created under the `dist` directory. The `dist` directory will be created for you if it does not already exist. Then the app.less file is compiled into `main.css`, which is then written to `dist/styles/main.css`.

Now `main.css` may be inspected to view the compiled result:

```
/* app css stylesheet */
.menu {
    color: #6794c3;
    border-color: #d6e1ed;
    -webkit-box-shadow: 0 0 5px #5B83AD;
    box-shadow: 0 0 5px #5B83AD;
}
```

```
.menu:before {
  content: «[«;
}
.menu:after {
  content: «]»;
}
.menu > li {
  display: inline;
}
.menu > li:before {
  content: "|";
  padding-right: 0.3em;
}
.menu > li:nth-child(1):before {
  content: "";
  padding: 0;
}
```

Modify the `index.html` file to use the newly generated CSS created by the LESS task. Simply comment out the existing import and add the new import as follows:

```
12    <link rel="stylesheet" href="bower_components/html5-boilerplate/dist/css/normalize.css">
13    <link rel="stylesheet" href="bower_components/html5-boilerplate/dist/css/main.css">
14    <!--link rel="stylesheet" href="app.css"-->
15    <link rel="stylesheet" href="../../dist/styles/main.css">
16    <script src="bower_components/html5-boilerplate/dist/js/vendor/modernizr-2.8.3.min.js"></script>
```

Now navigate to `http://localhost:8000/app/#/view1` and view the style change to the menu, which now has a light blue box-shadow style:

[view1 | view2]

This is the partial for view 1.

Angular seed app: v0.1

The new directory structure will now look as follows:

Testing the contrib-imagemin configuration

The process for testing the imagemin configuration will be extremely simple. We will need to create a directory for the images that will be used in sample_project and then add some test source images into the directory. We can get the images from the SpaceX public domain image site located at: `https://www.flickr.com/photos/spacexphotos`. Choose any photos you like and as many as you wish to use. This example will use the following two images:

`https://www.flickr.com/photos/spacexphotos/23802553412/`

`https://www.flickr.com/photos/spacexphotos/23604164970/`

First, create a directory named `images` located within the app directory. The path will be `sample_project/app/images`. Then, download the full-size Original source files from the SpaceX photos into the newly created `images` directory:

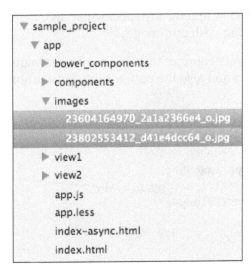

During the writing of this section, a bug was found in the version of contrib-imagemin being used. It was necessary to run an update of imagemin from version 0.9.4 to 1.0.1. This is accomplished by the following process:

In the terminal, issue the following command in order to get the current versions and any available updates to existing packages in the project:

`npm outdated`

This will provide output similar to this example:

```
Package                   Current   Wanted   Latest   Location
bower                       1.7.1    1.7.2    1.7.2    bower
grunt-contrib-uglify        0.9.2    0.9.2    0.11.0   grunt-contrib-uglify
http-server                 0.6.1    0.6.1    0.8.5    http-server
karma                     0.12.37  0.12.37   0.13.16  karma
karma-chrome-launcher      0.1.12   0.1.12    0.2.2    karma-chrome-launcher
karma-junit-reporter        0.2.2    0.2.2    0.3.8    karma-junit-reporter
protractor                  2.5.1    2.5.1    3.0.0    protractor
shelljs                     0.2.6    0.2.6    0.5.3    shelljs
```

Then, using the version found in the **Latest** column of the output, update the version number used in package.json. In this case the modification was to update imagemin registration in devDependencies to 1.0.0, as follows:

`"grunt-contrib-imagemin": "^1.0.0",`

Finally, running the npm command to update grunt-contrib-imagemin will then get the version from package.json and update the package in the node_modules directory:

`npm update grunt-contrib-imagemin`

This process may be used to update any specific package manually. Now we can return to testing imagemin with our images.

Next, modify the imagemin configuration in Gruntfile.js to point to the correct path for the source image files and also the path for the distribution directory, as follows:

```
imagemin: {
    dynamic: {
      files: [{
        expand: true,
        cwd: 'app/images/',
        src: ['**/*.{png,jpg,gif}'],
        dest: 'dist/images/'
      }]
    }
},
```

Notice that the `src` property configuration is a glob of file extensions that may be used for matching an expression to files in the source directory. The source directory is relative to the configuration for the **Current Working Directory (cwd)**, which is `app/images/`. Then the destination directory path is defined as the location where optimized images will be written.

Save your changes and then run the following command to run the imagemin task:

`grunt testing:imagemin`

```
drcsoft-mbp:sample_project dougrdotnet$ grunt testing:imagemin
Running "testing:imagemin" (testing) task

Running "imagemin:dynamic" (imagemin) task
Minified 2 images (saved 67.95 kB)

Done, without errors.
```

For these two images, imagemin reports that a total of `67.95 kB` was saved in optimization. The `images` directory was dynamically created on the first run. Now that the task has been run, the directory tree will be as follows:

```
▼ sample_project
  ▶ app
  ▶ bck_node_modules
  ▼ dist
    ▼ images
        23604164970_2a1a2366e4_o.jpg
        23802553412_d41e4dcc64_o.jpg
    ▶ scripts
    ▶ styles
```

Testing the notify configuration

The `notify` configuration is very simple; all that is needed is to declare the tasks and define the notification title and message. The title and task messages may be any text you wish to be displayed in the notification.

For the sample_project notify configuration, the following was used:

```
notify: {
    jshint: {
        options: {
```

```
          title: 'Linting Complete',
          message: 'jshint finished',
        }
      },
      uglify: {
        options: {
          title: 'Minification Complete',
          message: 'JavaScript is minified'
        }
      },
      less: {
        options: {
          title: 'LESS Compiled',
          message: 'CSS is generated'
        }
      },
      imagemin: {
        options: {
          title: 'Images Minified',
          message: 'Images are minified'
        }
      },
      watch: {
        options: {
          title: 'Watch Started',
          message: 'Watch is running'
        }
      }
    },
```

A small modification needs to be made to our `registerTask` callback in Gruntfile.
js: an additional parameter needs to be added to the function and that argument
variable needs to be added to the array of tasks in the `run` method. The modification
will look like this when complete:

```
grunt.registerTask('testing', 'testing individual tasks', function(a,
b) {
    grunt.task.run([a,b]);
  });
```

This will now allow us to run two tasks, passing both in one Terminal command
like this:

```
grunt testing:jshint:notify
```

In this example, both `jshint` and `notify` were run in a single command. `jshint` was passed into argument `a` and `notify` was passed into argument `b`. Then, `jshint` was run first with `notify` being run following the successful completion of `jshint`. The terminal output from this test should look like the following:

```
drcsoft-mbp:sample_project dougrdotnet$ grunt testing:jshint:notify
Running "testing:jshint:notify" (testing) task

Running "jshint:files" (jshint) task
>> 5 files lint free.

Running "jshint:gruntfile" (jshint) task
>> 1 file lint free.

Running "notify:jshint" (notify) task

Running "notify:uglify" (notify) task

Running "notify:less" (notify) task

Running "notify:imagemin" (notify) task

Running "notify:watch" (notify) task

Done, without errors.
```

The `notify` command will create a system notification using the configured title and message for each task defined within `notify`. For this example, growl is being used on this system, so the notification appears on screen and looks like the following:

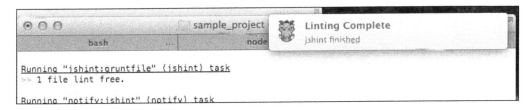

This is a really convenient feature because, when the sample_project automated build is fully configured, the build process will not need user interaction for each change. The process will launch automatically and the notifications will provide information about the task process. If there is an error, an error message will be included in the notification instead of the user-configured message:

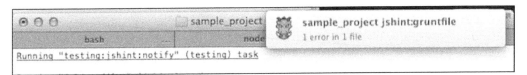

Upon notification, information may be obtained from the terminal about the error. Otherwise, you, the developer, don't have to monitor the terminal for each build.

Testing the open configuration

The open command is the simplest configuration of all the tasks that are being used in sample_project. All that is needed is to define the URL to open when the task is run along with the browser application name that should open the URL:

```
open : {
   dev : {
      path: 'http://localhost:8000/app/index.HTML',
      app: 'Google Chrome'
   }
},
```

In the case of sample_project, the HTTP server runs on localhost port 8000, with the homepage located in the path /app/index.HTML. The open command is configured to open Google Chrome in this example. No changes to Gruntfile.js are necessary at this time; simply run the following command for our setup used in notify, passing in two task arguments with the second one being open:

```
grunt testing:jshint:open
```

Once run, and assuming there are no errors in the jshint task for this example, the open command will launch Google Chrome and run the current version of sample_project in the running browser.

Testing the contrib-watch Configuration

The watch is the task that brings everything together for our truly automated build. Once configured, watch will continue running after the first manual build and automatically build when any of the configured files it is watching change. watch will also run any tasks configured to run when it detects changes in files. For sample_project, watch configuration should include any files that require other tasks to be run when files have been changed. The watch configuration will be configured like this:

```
watch: {
   gruntfile: {
      files: 'Gruntfile.js',
      tasks: ['jshint'],
   },
   scripts: {
```

```
     files:['app/app.js', 'app/view1/*.js', 'app/view2/*.js', 'app/
app.less'],
     tasks: ['default']
   }
},
```

In this configuration, if Gruntfile.js itself changes, then it should be linted to ensure no errors are introduced. Additionally, if any defined scripts change then the default task should be run. The default task configuration needs to be changed in order to include all of the tasks needed to run by default for sample_project. The `registerTask` method changes will look like the following:

```
grunt.registerTask('default',['jshint','uglify', 'less', 'imagemin',
'notify', 'open', 'watch']);
```

Running the default task only takes a single command from Terminal:

`grunt`

Once the default command runs for the first time, `watch` will continue to run and monitor for changes. The output for sample_project's first run will look like this example:

```
drcsoft-mbp:sample_project dougrdotnet$ grunt
Running "jshint:files" (jshint) task
>> 5 files lint free.

Running "jshint:gruntfile" (jshint) task
>> 1 file lint free.

Running "uglify:dist" (uglify) task
>> 1 file created.

Running "less:dist" (less) task
>> 1 stylesheet created.

Running "imagemin:dynamic" (imagemin) task
Minified 2 images (saved 67.95 kB)

Running "notify:jshint" (notify) task

Running "notify:uglify" (notify) task

Running "notify:less" (notify) task

Running "notify:imagemin" (notify) task

Running "notify:watch" (notify) task

Running "open:dev" (open) task

Running "watch" task
Waiting...
```

Next, make a small change to Gruntfile that adds an error. Remove a semi-colon, for example. Once saved, an error notification will be presented from `notify`. Inspect the terminal for the error:

```
Running "watch" task
Waiting...
>> File "Gruntfile.js" changed.
Running "jshint:files" (jshint) task
>> 5 files lint free.

Running "jshint:gruntfile" (jshint) task

   Gruntfile.js
     99 |  })
                 ^ Missing semicolon.

>> 1 error in 1 file
Warning: Task "jshint:gruntfile" failed. Use --force to continue.

Aborted due to warnings.
```

Revert the change made to Gruntfile.js so that there will be no errors and save the file:

```
Running "watch" task
Waiting...
>> File "Gruntfile.js" changed.
Running "jshint:files" (jshint) task
>> 5 files lint free.

Running "jshint:gruntfile" (jshint) task
>> 1 file lint free.

Done, without errors.
```

Notice that `notify` did not run now that there was no error. This is because `watch` does not specify `notify` to run when only Gruntfile.js is changed. Next, we will make a change to one of the files configured in the scripts property of `watch`. This time it is expected that the default task will run, launching all of our configured tasks. Open up app.js and place a comment at the top of the file:

```
'use strict';
// comment added for testing
// Declare app level module which depends on views, and components
angular.module('myApp', [
  'ngRoute',
  'myApp.view1',
  'myApp.view2',
```

```
    'myApp.version'
]).
config(['$routeProvider', function($routeProvider) {
  $routeProvider.otherwise({redirectTo: '/view1'});
}]);
```

Save the change and then notice that the default task runs automatically.
A notification will be presented for each task and the terminal output will provide
logging for the completion of each task. `watch` will continue to monitor for changes
and you can continue working without having to manually run any of your tasks:

```
>> File "app/app.js" changed.
Running "jshint:files" (jshint) task
>> 5 files lint free.

Running "jshint:gruntfile" (jshint) task
>> 1 file lint free.

Running "uglify:dist" (uglify) task
>> 1 file created.

Running "less:dist" (less) task
>> 1 stylesheet created.

Running "imagemin:dynamic" (imagemin) task
Minified 2 images (saved 67.95 kB)

Running "notify:jshint" (notify) task

Running "notify:uglify" (notify) task

Running "notify:less" (notify) task

Running "notify:imagemin" (notify) task

Running "notify:watch" (notify) task

Running "open:dev" (open) task

Running "watch" task
Waiting...
```

The Complete Gruntfile.js

Lets have a look at the code for the Gruntfile.js file:

```
module.exports = function(grunt) {
  'use strict';

  grunt.initConfig({
    // Metadata.
```

```
    pkg: grunt.file.readJSON('package.json'),
    banner: '/*! *** DO NOT EDIT THIS FILE ***\n' +
    'It is automatically generated in the build \n' +
    '<%= pkg.name %> - v<%= pkg.version %> - ' +
      '<%= grunt.template.today("yyyy-mm-dd") %>\n' +
      '<%= pkg.repository %>\n' +
      '* Copyright (c) <%= grunt.template.today("yyyy") %> <%= pkg.
author.name %>;*/\n',
    // Task configuration.
    jshint: {
      files: ['app/app.js', 'app/view1/*.js', 'app/view2/*.js'],
      options: {
          jshintrc: '.jshintrc'
        },
      gruntfile: {
        src: 'Gruntfile.js'
      }
    },
    uglify: {
      options: {
        banner: '<%= banner %>'
      },
      dist: {
        src: ['app/app.js', 'app/view1/view1.js', 'app/view2/view2.
js'],
        dest: 'dist/scripts/<%= pkg.name %>.<%= pkg.version %>.min.js'
      },
    },
    less: {
      options: {
        paths: ["app"]
      },
      dist: {
        src: 'app/app.less',
        dest: 'dist/styles/main.css'
      }
    },
    imagemin: {
      dynamic: {
        files: [{
          expand: true,
          cwd: 'app/images/',
          src: ['**/*.{png,jpg,gif}'],
          dest: 'dist/images/'
```

```
      }]
    }
  },
  notify: {
    jshint: {
      options: {
        title: 'Linting Complete',
        message: 'jshint finished',
      }
    },
    uglify: {
      options: {
        title: 'Minification Complete',
        message: 'JavaScript is minified'
      }
    },
    less: {
      options: {
        title: 'LESS Compiled',
        message: 'CSS is generated'
      }
    },
    imagemin: {
      options: {
        title: 'Images Minified',
        message: 'Images are minified'
      }
    },
    watch: {
      options: {
        title: 'Watch Started',
        message: 'Watch is running'
      }
    }
  },
  open : {
    dev : {
      path: 'http://localhost:8000/app/index.HTML',
      app: 'Google Chrome'
    }
  },
  watch: {
    gruntfile: {
      files: 'Gruntfile.js',
```

```
      tasks: ['jshint'],
    },
    scripts: {
      files:['app/app.js', 'app/view1/*.js', 'app/view2/*.js', 'app/
app.less'],
      tasks: ['default']
    }
  },
});

grunt.loadNpmTasks('grunt-contrib-jshint');
grunt.loadNpmTasks('grunt-contrib-uglify');
grunt.loadNpmTasks('grunt-contrib-less');
grunt.loadNpmTasks('grunt-contrib-imagemin');
grunt.loadNpmTasks('grunt-contrib-watch');
grunt.loadNpmTasks('grunt-notify');
grunt.loadNpmTasks('grunt-open');

grunt.registerTask('default',['jshint','uglify', 'less', 'imagemin',
'notify', 'open', 'watch']);

};
```

Summary

In this chapter, we learned the process of loading tasks. We added them incrementally so they could be checked to ensure the expected results were being generated. Custom and default tasks were created in order to automate the build process, the default task allowed us to create a launch configuration. This required only a single command from Terminal to start up our automated build. In the next chapter, we will explore the creation of a more advanced custom task.

7
Advanced Grunt Concepts

In this chapter, we will look at an advanced Grunt concept—the creation and implementation of a custom task. In *Chapter 6, Building the Sample Project* we looked at how we can create custom tasks in `Gruntfile.js`; now, we will look at writing a task that will be implemented and used like any of the other tasks that we have been working with throughout the book. We will write a custom task that will reside in the tasks directory, create a configuration in `Gruntfile.js`, and load and register the custom task. For this plugin, a gzip task will be created to illustrate how you can build and implement your own tasks. You may find it very difficult to come up with a need that has not already been met with an existing plugin created to solve the same problem. Always search NPM for existing plugins. For the rare case that you are unable to find a plugin to meet your needs, this chapter will help you grasp the scope of what needs to be done.

The topic that we are going to cover is as follows:

*   Creating a Grunt plugin

Creating a Grunt plugin

We will be using grunt-init, which is a scaffolding tool.

Using the Grunt plugin scaffold

Grunt provides you with a plugin module creation with grunt-init-gruntplugin, which will scaffold your plugin authoring environment. While using gruntplugin is not mandatory, it is recommended by the Grunt team. The gruntplugin requires grunt-init to be installed. Clone grunt-init-gruntplugin from its repository:

```
git clone git://github.com/gruntjs/grunt-init-gruntplugin.git ~/.grunt-
init/gruntplugin.
```

In Windows, the destination path should be modified to `%USERPROFILE%\.grunt-init\gruntplugin`.

Alternatively, navigate to `https://github.com/gruntjs/grunt-init-gruntplugin`, where you can download the plugin files, and then place the template in your `~/.grunt-init` directory. Once the template has been added, run the following from the directory where you wish to author your plugin:

cd path/to/plugin_directory

grunt-init gruntplugin

The output is as follows:

```
drcsoft-mbp:plugins dougrdotnet$ grunt-init gruntplugin
Running "init:gruntplugin" (init) task
This task will create one or more files in the current directory, based on the
environment and the answers to a few questions. Note that answering "?" to any
question will show question-specific help and answering "none" to most questions
will leave its value blank.

"gruntplugin" template notes:
For more information about Grunt plugin best practices, please see the docs at
http://gruntjs.com/creating-plugins

Please answer the following:
[?] Project name (grunt-plugins) grunt-gz
[?] Description (The best Grunt plugin ever.) Grunt gzip task
[?] Version (0.1.0) 0.1.0
[?] Project git repository (git://github.com/dougrdotnet/plugins.git) https://gi
thub.com/DougReynolds/grunt-gz.git
[?] Project homepage (https://github.com/DougReynolds/grunt-gz) https://github.c
om/DougReynolds/grunt-gz
[?] Project issues tracker (https://github.com/DougReynolds/grunt-gz/issues) htt
ps://github.com/DougReynolds/grunt-gz/issues
[?] Licenses (MIT) MIT
[?] Author name (Douglas Reynolds) Douglas Reynolds
[?] Author email (                    ) none
[?] Author url (none) https://dougreynolds.github.io/
[?] What versions of grunt does it require? (~0.4.5) ~0.4.5
[?] What versions of node does it run on? (>= 0.8.0) >=0.12.7
[?] Do you need to make any changes to the above before continuing? (y/N) N

Writing .gitignore...OK
Writing .jshintrc...OK
Writing Gruntfile.js...OK
Writing README.md...OK
Writing tasks/gz.js...OK
Writing test/expected/custom_options...OK
Writing test/expected/default_options...OK
Writing test/fixtures/123...OK
Writing test/fixtures/testing...OK
Writing test/gz_test.js...OK
Writing LICENSE-MIT...OK
Writing package.json...OK

Initialized from template "gruntplugin".
You should now install project dependencies with npm install. After that, you
may execute project tasks with grunt. For more information about installing
and configuring Grunt, please see the Getting Started guide:

http://gruntjs.com/getting-started

Done, without errors.
```

Following the illustration of the preceding screenshot, initializing the gruntplugin will involve answering a series of questions. The answers to these questions will populate a newly created `package.json` in the root of the plugin root directory. Additionally, the plugin directory structure will be created:

Finally, run the `npm install` command:

```
drcsoft-mbp:plugins dougrdotnet$ npm install
npm WARN package.json grunt-gz@0.1.0 No license field.
npm WARN deprecated lodash@0.9.2: lodash@<2.0.0 is no longer maintained. Upgrade
 to lodash@^3.0.0
grunt-contrib-clean@0.5.0 node_modules/grunt-contrib-clean
└── rimraf@2.2.8

grunt@0.4.5 node_modules/grunt
├── which@1.0.9
├── dateformat@1.0.2-1.2.3
├── eventemitter2@0.4.14
├── getobject@0.1.0
├── rimraf@2.2.8
├── colors@0.6.2
├── async@0.1.22
├── hooker@0.2.3
├── grunt-legacy-util@0.2.0
├── exit@0.1.2
├── nopt@1.0.10 (abbrev@1.0.7)
├── minimatch@0.2.14 (sigmund@1.0.1, lru-cache@2.7.3)
├── glob@3.1.21 (inherits@1.0.2, graceful-fs@1.2.3)
├── lodash@0.9.2
├── coffee-script@1.3.3
├── underscore.string@2.2.1
├── iconv-lite@0.2.11
├── findup-sync@0.1.3 (glob@3.2.11, lodash@2.4.2)
├── grunt-legacy-log@0.1.3 (grunt-legacy-log-utils@0.1.1, underscore.string@2.3.
3, lodash@2.4.2)
└── js-yaml@2.0.5 (argparse@0.1.16, esprima@1.0.4)

grunt-contrib-jshint@0.9.2 node_modules/grunt-contrib-jshint
├── hooker@0.2.3
└── jshint@2.4.4 (console-browserify@0.1.6, exit@0.1.2, underscore@1.4.4, minima
tch@0.4.0, shelljs@0.1.4, cli@0.4.5, htmlparser2@3.3.0)

grunt-contrib-nodeunit@0.3.3 node_modules/grunt-contrib-nodeunit
└── nodeunit@0.8.8 (tap@5.1.2)
```

For the preceding example, there is no concern for the warnings provided in the NPM initialization. At this point, you are ready to begin writing your Grunt plugin.

Authoring a custom plugin

Once you have completed the gruntplugin scaffolding process, you will have a pregenerated task, package.json, and Gruntfile.js along with other directories and files for node modules, test, gitignore, license, and readme files. The `grunt-contrib-jshint` file is installed by default in this process, so a `.jshintrc` file is also created. Additionally, grunt-contrib-clean and grunt-contrib-nodeunit are installed in the process:

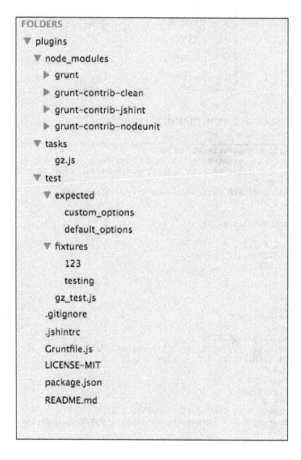

The purpose of the plugin for this example will be to Gzip folders within a source directory and output compressed files to a deployment preparation directory. For this purpose, we will need two node.js libraries: zlib, which will provide the actual gzip functionality, and fs, which will provide file system methods needed by the plugin. We can begin modifying the scaffold for the plugin needs by navigating to the tasks directory in the plugin root and opening gz.js in the editor. Note that the scaffold created a working plugin that will concatenate two files. We will go ahead and remove this code and build up the gz task. Begin by removing all the code from within the registerMultiTask method:

```js
gz.js                    ●    Gruntfile.js          ×
 1   /*
 2    * grunt-gz
 3    * https://github.com/DougReynolds/grunt-gz
 4    *
 5    * Copyright (c) 2016 Douglas Reynolds
 6    * Licensed under the MIT license.
 7    */
 8
 9   'use strict';
10
11   module.exports = function(grunt) {
12
13       // Please see the Grunt documentation for more information regarding task
14       // creation: http://gruntjs.com/creating-tasks
15
16       grunt.registerMultiTask('gz', 'Grunt gzip task', function() {
17
18       });
19
20   };
21
```

The task itself is not the main point of this chapter, rather, the process of creating a custom task and implementation in your project is. For this reason, the coding process will be skimmed through so that focus can remain on custom task creation.

The following is the plugin code in its entirety:

```js
/*
 * grunt-gz
 * https://github.com/DougReynolds/grunt-gz
 *
 * Copyright (c) 2016 Douglas Reynolds
 * Licensed under the MIT license.
 */

'use strict';

var zlib = require( 'zlib' );
```

```
var fs = require( 'fs' );

module.exports = function( grunt ) {
  grunt.registerMultiTask( 'gz', 'Grunt gzip task', function() {
    var gzip = zlib.createGunzip();
    var processComplete = this.async();

    // create sourceFiles array and populate it
    var sourceFiles = [];
    grunt.file.recurse( grunt.config.get( 'gz.files.source' ),
function( abspath, rootdir, subdir, filename ){
      sourceFiles.push( filename );
    });

    // Async function which obtains files from source directory
    //   configuration and archives them in gzip format to a
    //   distribution directory.
    function gzip_sourceFiles() {
      // Check sourceFiles array to see if any files left to process
      if( sourceFiles.length <= 0 ) {
        processComplete();
        return;
      }

      // set value to removed file from array
      var srcFile = sourceFiles.pop();

      // the source distribution directories
      var src = grunt.config.get( 'gz.files.source' );
      var dist = grunt.config.get( 'gz.files.dist' );

      // create the distribution directory if it does not exist
      if ( !fs.existsSync( dist ) ){
        fs.mkdirSync( dist );
      } else {
        // recurse the distribution directory to check for hidden
files
        grunt.file.recurse( dist, function( abspath, rootdir, subdir,
filename ){
          // skip hidden files
          if ( filename.indexOf( '.' ) === 0 ) {
            console.log( 'Hidden file ' + filename );
            gzip_sourceFiles();
            return;
```

```
        }
      });
    }


    // the file to be gzipped
    var fileToZip = grunt.file.read( src + '/' + srcFile, {
encoding: null } );

    if ( srcFile.indexOf( '.' ) === 0 ) {
      console.log( 'hidden file 2 ' + srcFile );
      gzip_sourceFiles();
      return;
    }

    grunt.log.writeln( "Compressing " + srcFile + " ..." );

    // zlib gzip method to compress the file and write to
distribution directory
    zlib.gzip( fileToZip, function( err, gzipped ) {
        grunt.file.write( dist + '/' + srcFile + '.gz', gzipped );
        grunt.log.ok( "Compressed file written to " + dist );

        // recursively call ourself
        gzip_sourceFiles();
      });
    }
    // start the gzip process
    gzip_sourceFiles();
  });

};
```

Here is a brief walk-through. The comments in the code further document what is going on so have a look there for specifics too. At the top, we require zlib and fs so that these libraries are available to us in the task. Within the registerMultiTask method, the gzip function is declared as a variable and the grunt asynchronous method is defined. This will provide us with asynchronous behavior and calling this method will notify Grunt that the asynchronous task has been completed. Just below this is Grunt's recurse method to recurse through the source files and create an array of files.

Next, we define the task method. This is where the body of the gzip work will occur; it includes control logic, fetching source files, and writing compressed files. If there are no files in the source directory, we end the process immediately; otherwise, the task continues and pops a file from the sourcefile array and assigns it to a variable. We define the source and distribution directories obtained from the Gruntfile configuration. A quick check is done to see if the distribution directory already exists, if not, the directory is created. Note that this task does not handle cleanup. Using another plugin, such as clean, would be needed to remove the distribution directory and/or files prior to running this task. Some defensive code is added to protect against existing hidden files should the directory exist without previously Gzipped files.

Finally, the file to be compressed is defined and checked to ensure that it is not a hidden file. If the file is an expected source file, then the zlib gzip method is called to compress the file, which is then written to the distribution directory. The task calls itself recursively and a check at the beginning of the method determines if there are more files to compress. If not, the task completes.

The last part of creating the plugin is the setting up in the Gruntfile configuration, loading the task, and registering it to run. When grunt-init-gruntplugin was run, a Gruntfile and package.json were also created. There should be no additional modifications necessary to package.json; however, Gruntfile.js will require configuration to provide source and distribution locations to the task. This is done simply as follows:

```
gz: {
  files: {
    source:'/path/to/source/directory',
    dist:'/path/to/destination/directory'
  }
},
```

For information on defining source and destination paths, see the Grunt Files API, `http://gruntjs.com/configuring-tasks#files`. The preceding example is provided as a simplified example for the purpose of this task. Then, we are ready to complete the setup of the task by loading the task:

```
grunt.loadTasks('tasks');
```

Then, we register the task to run:

```
grunt.registerTask('default', ['jshint', 'gz']);
```

Finally, with an actual source and distribution path defined, the task can be run from Terminal with the `grunt` command:

```
drcsoft-mbp:plugins dougrdotnet$ grunt
Running "jshint:all" (jshint) task
>> 3 files lint free.

Running "gz:files" (gz) task
Compressing main.js ...
>> Compressed file written to /Users/dougrdotnet/Desktop/grunt_test/deploy
hidden file 2 .DS_Store

Done, without errors.
```

A final, optional step would be to submit your plugin to NPM for publishing in the NPM registry. This is done simply with the `npm publish` command.

Once your plugin exists in the NPM registry, it is available to be installed with NPM just like any other plugin. This can be done simply with the `npm-install [plugin-name]` command.

Summary

Rolling your own custom tasks provides you with the means to be as expressive in providing solutions to task automation needs as you wish. Grunt provides the scaffolding to get up and running quickly, allowing you to focus on building your plugin. It is highly likely that another developer has encountered the same type of problem and a solution already exists in the NPM registry. If not, then building your own is definitely within reach. It is a steep, but short, learning curve from entry to publishing your plugin. There is a great deal of information available as well as examples throughout the NPM registry and GitHub. Check out the gruntplugin tool at `http://gruntjs.com/creating-plugins`. Then, read through the generated concatenation plugin code and documentation to get started.

Have fun!

Index

Symbols

$PATH variable
  Node.js installation path, adding to 15-17
.msi
  used, for upgrading Node.js on
      Windows 9, 10
  URL 9

A

Angular Seed Project
  application, running 38, 39
  cloning 30, 31
  creating 29, 40
  dependencies 30
  dependencies, installing 32-37
  installing 39
  references 29
  URL 40

C

Change Directory (cd) command 16
command line interface (CLI) 2
contrib-clean plugin 58, 59
contrib-concat plugin 57, 58
contrib-cssmin plugin 56, 57
contrib-htmlmin plugin 59, 60
contrib-imagemin plugin
  about 53
  configuration, testing 138-141
contrib-jshint plugin
  about 47, 48
  configuration, testing 128-131
  installing, with NPM 66-68

contrib-less plugin
  about 50, 51
  configuration, testing 133-138
  installing, with NPM 70, 71
contrib-uglify plugin
  about 49, 50
  configuration, testing 131-133
  installing, with NPM 68, 69
contrib-watch plugin
  about 60-62
  configuration, testing 144-147
  installing, with NPM 71
Current Working Directory (CWD) 102, 141
custom task configuration 126, 127

D

default task configuration 124, 125
dependencies
  about 2
  Node.js 2, 3
  Node Package Manager (NPM) 2, 3
devDependencies object looping method
  using 121-124
developer tools
  URL 34
downloaded binary
  used, for installing Node.js 10-14

E

ES6 Module Syntax page
  URL 85
event API 86

J

jshint
about 2
URL 48, 61
json file
URL 46

L

Less 2
LoadNpmTasks method
used, for calling plugins 120, 121
using 120
log API 89

M

Mac
Node.js, upgrading via NPM 6-8

N

newer plugin 54
Node.js
about 4
downloading 5
installation path, adding to $PATH
variable 15-17
installing 5, 6
installing, via downloaded binary 10-14
upgrading 5, 6
upgrading, on Windows via .msi
and NPM 9, 10
upgrading, via NPM on Mac 6-8
URL 5
Node Package Manager (NPM)
about 1, 4, 111
downloading 5
Node.js, upgrading on Mac 6-8
Node.js, upgrading on Windows 9, 10
updating, for Grunt CLI 18
URL 5
used, for installing Grunt CLI 18
node-semver
URL 74

notify configuration

testing 141-144
notify plugin 51, 52
npm directory
URL 66
NPM documentation
URL 76
NPM glob project
URL 88
NPM grunt-newer plugin documentation
URL 112
NPM jshint documentation
URL 109

O

open configuration
testing 144
open plugin 52
option API 89, 90

P

package.json file 73-75

S

sample_project
requisites 93
slide deck 96-99
SSH plugin 55, 56
strip-json-comments
URL 66
Subversion (SVN) 22

T

task API 90, 91
task loading
about 119
devDependencies object looping
method, using 121-124
plugins calling, loadNpmTasks
method used 120, 121
template API 90

U

Uglify 2
unofficial plugins
  concurrent 3
  newer 3
  notify 3
  open 3
user stories 94

W

Watch 2
Windows
  Node.js, upgrading via .msi and NPM 9, 10

Y

Yeoman
  URL 21